For the Love of Poetry

Literacy Scaffolds, Extension Ideas, and More

For the Love of Poetry

Literacy Scaffolds, Extension Ideas, and More

NANCY LEE CECIL

PEGUIS
PUBLISHERS

WINNIPEG • MANITOBA • CANADA

Printed and bound in Canada by Hignell Printing Limited

01 02 03 4 3 2

Canadian Cataloguing in Publication Data

Cecil, Nancy Lee

    For the love of poetry

    Includes bibliographical references
    ISBN 1-895411-87-4

1. Poetry – Study and teaching (Elementary).
2. Poetry – Study and teaching (Secondary).   I. Title.

LB1576.C44 1997   372.6   C97-920126-8

Book and Cover Design: David Ashcroft
Text Illustrations: Pamela Dixon
Cover Illustration: Ken Stampnick

Peguis Publishers
100-318 McDermot Avenue
Winnipeg, Manitoba
Canada R3A 0A2

Toll free: 1-800-667-9673
E-mail: books@peguis.com
Visit our web site: http://www.ideasforteachers.com

To my favorite poet, Chrissy

Contents

Acknowledgments

I would like to give a hearty thanks to all my friends, students, colleagues, and family members who so eagerly tried out these scaffolds, shared their poems, and gave me helpful feedback. This book, with their help, was pure joy to put together.

I must also express gratitude to my editor, Leigh Hambly, who has always managed to share the same vision I do for writing poetry in this stressfree fashion. I feel privileged, too, to be working with the Dixon family who offer a refreshing personal touch to publishing a book. A special thanks to all of you.

Finally, I wish to thank my husband Gary and lovely daughter Chrissy, who are always there to listen, support, and encourage.

Introduction

The nature of elementary and middle school populations in North America has changed considerably since most of today's adults were in school. In general, elementary and middle school student bodies are more diverse; a trend projected to continue well into the twenty-first century. Likely, the proportion of children from single-parent households will also continue to increase. The percentage of children belonging to ethnic and linguistic minorities will continue to grow. William Teale (1989) describes today's school population as a "...rich, vibrant mosaic—a dynamic composite of children from a variety of cultures, linguistic backgrounds, and religions."

In the past thirty years children have been profoundly affected by the changes in society, family structures, the increased mobility among families, and technology. The very nature of childhood and the ways children learn and come to know about the world are different. Some feel the "magic" of childhood has been denied to a whole new generation of children.

What are the implications of all this for the teacher of the language arts? Lucy Calkins believes the early childhood, elementary, and middle school-level language arts curriculums could perhaps play a more critical role than ever before in children's education. Through the reading and sharing of children's literature and through the self-exploration and creative expression in language that it affords, children can perhaps regain some of the simple benefits and pleasures of unsophisticated play that we adults remember so nostalgically. Through sharing literature with children, teachers can hope to provide a small antidote for some of the negative influences increasingly surrounding our children (Calkins 1991).

As children's ideas, lives, and stories are valued alongside the ideas, lives, and stories of their classmates, they can achieve a greater measure of empowerment and validation—the nurturing ingredients in healthy development. Effective teaching of language arts can have an impact on children's lives far beyond that of developing literacy skills.

Language arts—if it is directed toward the child's heart and soul—can make a major difference in the lives of children. The ideal component of the language arts to reach the heart and soul of learners is poetry.

Why Poetry?

Poetry can best be described as "a design of words" or, as one poet aptly mused, "painting with words." The fresh, whimsical ways most children think, talk, and write make them naturally good at this artistic endeavor. As most observers of children's language will attest, children are "natural" poets. Additionally, when children are allowed to experiment with language, they learn to construct meaning and make sense of their world. The free and imaginative vehicle of poetry is, for many children, liberating. Poetry lets children speak and write freely in their own special language.

Creating a Poetry Curriculum

Unfortunately, too many students have been systematically "turned off" poetry. The reasons are many. They may have been taught by well-meaning, enthusiastic teachers who coerced them to explicate turgid, flowery poetry that failed to reach them on their level. They may have had teachers who were lukewarm to poetry themselves and either omitted this part of the language arts curriculum or addressed it in a rather halfhearted way. The good news is that poetry can easily be made highly enjoyable and accessible to all students—regardless of ability level or primary language. The following steps ensure a successful instructional program:

- Have the students write their own poetry, using the literacy scaffolds, or temporary writing structures, in this book.
- Select a variety of poetry books and anthologies and have them accessible for browsing and free reading times (see page 118, appendix B for suggestions).
- Read your favorite poems into a tape recorder. Then, create a poetry listening center where students can listen and follow along or record the poems they like best for others.

- Collect poems in a poetry file. During spare moments throughout the day, students can read an ode, limerick, or rap chant.
- Encourage poetry reading via a continuing game of "Poem in My Pocket." In this game, children are constantly on the lookout for poems that they like and wish to share. At recess or during special times of the day, classmates, teachers, or even guests in the classroom may ask any student, "What poem is in your pocket?" That student then reads his or her poem or asks the other person to do so.
- Help students compile their own anthologies of the poems they have written. Have the students illustrate and laminate their anthologies and circulate them around the classroom for others to read and enjoy.
- Culminate the poetry experience with a formal "Poetry Reading." Have the students read both their own original poetry and several poems from the works of published poets they admire. Make this event extra special by having the students use multimedia in their presentations. For example, students could use a slide show, puppets, special lighting, audience participation, posters, sound effects, and any other ideas to bring their poems to life.

Poetry Across the Curriculum

A special feature of this book is a plethora of ideas to extend the ideas children express in poetry throughout the curriculum. Teachers have long observed that children understand language more when it is integrated across the curriculum (Harste, Woodward & Burke 1984; King 1985; Lytle & Botel 1990; Wells 1986, 1988). Children speak, listen, read, and write as they conduct a science experiment; as they consider problems and discover patterns in math; as they engage in an inquiry in social studies; as they reflect on some art project; and on and on.

Because the content of each of these disciplines or curricular domains is different, children discover that they can use language (both oral and written) in many different ways. Communicative competence is enhanced in myriad ways. Metalinguistic and metacognitive awarenesses—the abilities to learn about language; to consider language as an object of study in and of itself; to ponder one's own thinking processes; to examine one's own strategies in approaching certain problems in science, or math, or social studies—are facilitated when children recognize that there are many different ways of perceiving and knowing the world.

Collaborative Learning in the Language Arts

Exercises in collaborative learning are another feature of this book. Teachers can divide the class into small groups for the poetry writing, or for the extended activities that follow. Children learn most effectively through collaboration with others (King 1985; Newman 1985; Wells 1986, 1988). Children in an integrated language classroom are supported linguistically, intellectually, and emotionally through their interactions with their peers. Rather than using individual "seat work" where talk is strictly forbidden, purposeful conversation among students is encouraged during poetry brainstorming and writing, as well as during the extended activities.

For example, after writing "I Dream" poems (see page 90), small groups of students could do a "dream survey" to investigate the sleeping habits of other students in the school. Some of the students in each group may be responsible for drawing up a list of the questions they will ask; others may decide whom to ask and when to ask them; and so forth. Decisions about individual contributions to the project require plenty of negotiation.

To understand and be understood is the basis of communication and of learning in general. Individual children have had varying experiences and, therefore, have different funds of knowledge on any particular topic. In addition, children have unique personal characteristics, and come from a variety of cultural and linguistic backgrounds. Such far-reaching diversity also means differing customs, interaction styles, and rules for communication. Because everyone's "way with words" will be different, all children can learn new ways to approach language through collaboration.

How to Use this Book

In the following pages the preservice and practicing teacher will find numerous poem ideas, or literacy scaffolds. The literacy scaffolds are clear, explicable structures that can be shown to students and then imitated by them so that they can easily write their own poetry, using their own ideas, experiences, and fresh perceptions of the world. Each poem idea includes a description that explains the structure that is to be imitated, and a lead-in activity to help the teacher get the students motivated and mentally set for the poetry writing session. Included with the poem idea are two example poems—original poems that have been created by real children in diverse classroom settings using the literacy scaffold. Some of the poem ideas are based on published poems by well-known poets (see page 117, appendix A for more information). The teacher can print each example poem on the chalkboard or overhead, read it chorally with the children, and then help children to identify the structure that is to be imitated. In some cases, no explanation is needed.

Each poem idea also contains three extended activities. These activities may be from the areas of art, social studies, math, science, physical education, or the language arts. Teachers can use the ideas as springboards for the entire curriculum. Many of the lesson ideas offered are for small group collaboration. These lessons will further enhance the sense of community in the classroom and provide more authentic purposes for communication among the children. The lessons have been specifically created with the linguistic needs of the second-language learner in mind.

Finally, this book is for teachers who are excited by the challenges of the "diverse mosaic" of students we now see in our classrooms, but who are struggling to better address the needs of these children and all others. Such teachers know that poetry has rich possibilities that other more rigid modes of discourse do not have. They know that poetry is indeed the universal language. The literacy scaffolds contained in this book will help to make this language flourish.

Literacy Scaffolds

❶ Cherished Item

(Adapted from *Umbilical* by Eve Merriam)

Description

This prescribed poem format focuses on a cherished item belonging to the poet. The poem addresses how difficult it would be for the poet to try to live without the item. The format is as follows:

You can take away my _____ ,
You can take away my _____ ,
But PLEASE don't take away
My [*adjective*] [*cherished item*].

I can do without _____ ,
I can do without _____ ,
But I can't do without
[*Phrase telling about cherished item*].

I can live without _____ ,
I can live without _____ ,
But I can't live without
My _____ .

Lead-in Activity

Ask students to imagine they have just been told their family is moving to a very small apartment. Other than their clothing, they will be allowed to bring only one personal cherished item (for example, a favorite toy, radio, computer, or a special book or game). Ask the students what they would bring and why. Invite them to share their answers with the rest of the class. Following this activity, read Eve Merriam's poem *Umbilical* (see page 117, appendix A for more information) aloud and discuss the child's favorite item. Next, read the following poems aloud. Then, discuss why the authors might have made the choices they did. Finally, have students write their own poems.

My Baseball Cap (Cherished Item #1)

You can take away my hamster,
You can take away my cat,
But PLEASE don't take away
My beloved baseball cap.

I can do without green,
I can do without red,
But I can't do without
My cap upon my head.

I can live without my house,
I can live without my school,
But I can't live without
My cap because it's cool.

—Neal, grade 4

My Parakeet (Cherished Item #2)

You can take away my soda,
You can take away food to eat,
But PLEASE don't take away
My precious parakeet.

I can do without play,
I can do without sleep,
But I can't do without
Hearing that bird peep.

I can live without new clothes,
I can live without the mall,
But I can't live without
My parakeet at all!

—Aron, grade 4

Science Extension

Discuss with students the four basic needs of humans (food, water, shelter, and air). Have students gather into small groups to prioritize these needs in what they would consider to be the *most* important to the *least* important. Have a spokesperson for each group report on his or her group's discussion to the rest of the class. Then provide factual information as to why the needs might be prioritized differently from what the groups postulated (for example, the fact that humans can live for only three minutes without air should top the list). Finally, discuss whether or not the cherished items that students wrote about are necessary for survival. Ask the students to consider: Why were none of the basic needs written about?

Art/Language Arts Extension

Distribute circular pieces of paper cut from white construction paper. Ask the students to draw a picture of their cherished item in the center of the paper. Then, have them write their poem in cursive writing around the edge of the circle, starting at the outer periphery of the paper.

Social Studies Extension

For each student in your class, bring in three identical items (for example, three toothpicks, three paper clips, three buttons, and so on). Give each student three different items. Then, write on the chalkboard all the items you have distributed. Next, tell the students to trade, or barter, one or more of their items for some other item(s) they would prefer. When they have done this, ask them: "Who was able to trade successfully?" "Who did not make a successful trade?" "Why were some of you not able to trade successfully?" Finally, discuss how and why we ascribe value to certain items and not to others. (Note: This discussion may lead to an introduction of the economic concept of "supply and demand.")

❷ Gift Poem

Description

This poem idea is adapted from the traditional poem and song *Mockingbird*, which has been handed down through the ages (see page 117, appendix A for more information). There are no set number of lines. Rhyming is optional, but fun. The poem format is as follows:

[*Name*], [*name*], have you heard (*or another similar question*)?
[*Name of benefactor*]'s going to buy me a [*gift*].
If that [*gift*] won't [*verb*],
[*Benefactor*]'s going to buy me a/an [*another gift*].
If that [*gift*] won't [*verb*],
[*Benefactor*]'s going to buy me a/an [*another gift*].
Repeat as often as desired.

Lead-in Activity

Have students tell about special presents they have received. List these on the chalkboard. Then ask if anyone has ever had to return a gift because there was something wrong with it. Ask them how they felt and how they avoided hurting the feelings of the person who gave them the gift.

Read the example poems. Then tell the students they are going to use the gifts listed on the chalkboard to play a game. Ask the first child to say to the person next to him or her, "[*Student's name*], have you heard? Daddy's going to buy me a [*gift*]." Allow that student to select a gift from the list on the chalkboard. Have the next student answer, "If that [*gift*] won't [*verb*], Daddy's going to buy me a [*another gift from list on chalkboard*]." Go around the room in this manner until the students have used all the words listed on the chalkboard or have run out of ideas. Then, encourage small groups of students to write a poem, using the format of the example poems.

Gift Poem #1

Joshua, Joshua, did you know?
Grandpa's going to buy me some arrows and a bow.
And if those arrows don't shoot straight,
Grandpa's going to buy me some fishing bait.
And if that bait won't catch any fish,
Grandpa's going to buy me anything I wish!

—*Mani & Jason, grade 6*

Gift Poem #2

Hey, Everybody, have you heard the news?
My mom's going to take me on a riverboat cruise.
And if that cruise is not much fun,
My mom's going to buy me a cinnamon bun.
And if that cinnamon bun's not okay,
My mom's going to buy me a flute to play.
And if that flute won't play a note,
My mom's going to put me back on that boat!

—*Svava & Ryan, grade 7*

Music Extension

Introduce the students to the traditional folk song, "Mockingbird," from which this poem idea was derived. Also try to obtain a copy of the adaptation of the song sung by Carly Simon and James Taylor. Using a matrix, chart the differences between the two songs in terms of style, rhythm, and word choices.

Language Arts Extension

Invite students to create stories from the poems they have written. Have them describe in detail the frustration they felt every time they had to exchange a gift. Encourage them to use realistic dialogue to bring to life the conversations they had with the salesclerk during the gift exchanges. Finally, have the students read their stories aloud in pairs. Have the author read the part of himself or herself and have the other student read the part of the salesclerk.

Art Extension

Pass out 11" x 14" (28 cm x 35.5 cm) sheets of colored construction paper and 8" x 10" sheets (20 cm x 25.5 cm) of white paper to the students. Ask them to pick the most "problematic" gift in their poem. Give them crayons or colored markers and have them draw a picture of that gift, along with the problem, greatly exaggerated, on the white paper. Then, have them cut out their pictures and glue them onto the bottom of the colored construction paper. Give each student a small gift bow to attach to their present. Finally, on the top half of the paper, have them glue an edited and revised copy of their "Gift Poem."

Something Told Them

(Adapted from *Something Told the Wild Geese* by Rachel Field)

Description

This four-stanza poem whimsically describes the process by which an animal makes the transition from one stage of development to another. It follows a unique structure that allows freedom of expression, yet provides subtle direction to ensure writer success. The format is as follows:

First stanza: Something told the [*noun*]
It was time to [*verb*].
Though [*phrase*],
[*Phrase; last word rhymes with verb on second line*].

Second stanza: Free verse

Third stanza: Free verse

Fourth stanza: Something told the [*noun*]
It was time to [*verb*].
[*Resolution*],
[*Resolution*].

Lead-in Activity

Have the students close their eyes. Ask them to visualize a caterpillar transforming itself into a butterfly. Invite them to imagine what the creature is thinking and feeling as it goes through each stage. Take them to the tree where the caterpillar is happily chewing away. Have them experience what the caterpillar is thinking as it begins spinning a cocoon. Then ask the students to try to imagine the insect's amazement as it emerges from the cocoon and flies as a butterfly for the very first time.

When the students open their eyes, invite them to tell about the experience as they imagined it. Ask: "Who told the caterpillar to spin the cocoon?" "Who told it when it was time to come out?" Read the following poems aloud, then have the students brainstorm other animals that go from one stage to another. Finally, have them write their own "Something Told Them" poem.

Something Told the Tadpole (Something Told Them #1)

Something told the tadpole
   His tail just had to go.
Though he liked being a little fish,
   Something told him, "Grow!"

His pond was nice and cozy,
   And he had just found a new friend.
But though his head was the same as always,
   He had a problem with his other end.

His body was really growing,
   And he thought he might explode.
He had a lot of nightmares,
   Of waking up as a toad.

Something told the tadpole
   There was a better life in store.
So he finally changed into a frog,
   And now sunbathes on the shore.

                 —*Carmen, grade 6*

Something Told the Baby (Something Told Them #2)

Something told the baby
   It was time for her to walk.
Though she enjoyed being treated like an infant,
   Someone whispered, "Talk!"

Her parents understood her cooing
   And she was crawling pretty well.
But when she had a secret
   It was hard for her to tell.

The whole wide world was waiting
For her first words to appear.
But when she said her first, "!@#$%!"
It wasn't very clear.

Something told the baby
It was time to say her mother's name.
She took a step and said, "Mama!"
Her life was never the same.
                                        —Anna, grade 6

Science Extension

Tell the students that, although they have been writing "whimsical poems" about animals being told to go through life stages, there is actually a scientific explanation for why these changes take place. Introduce the concept of "instinct." Discuss various animals for whom this concept applies. Some examples are the lemmings march to the sea; the geese and their yearly migrations; the snake shedding its skin; the caterpillar making a cocoon; the spider spinning a web. Have the students use CD-ROMs, encyclopedias, tradebooks, and other resources to help them find out as much as they can about the instinct that spurs an animal from one stage to the next.

Art Extension

For this activity, provide students with both black and white construction paper. Ask them to make one pencil drawing of the animal in their poem before it was "told" to change in a particular way and another pencil drawing to show how the animal looked after it had made the change. Have them do their "before" drawing on white construction paper, then cut it out and paste it onto the bottom of a half sheet of black construction paper. Then instruct them to draw their "after" picture on white construction paper and attach it to the top of a half sheet of black construction paper. Have students tape the two pieces of construction paper together and paste a final draft of their poem in the center of the two papers.

Language Arts Extension

Define the word *intuition*. Ask students to give examples of times when they felt they simply knew something was going to happen, or times when they didn't do something because they had a feeling something bad might happen. Discuss how this feeling relates to or differs from what the animals do in their poems. Invite them to write a paragraph telling about the feeling of intuition they had and what happened. Tell the students their pieces can be "pretend" or "real."

Measurement Poem

(Adapted from *How Many, How Much?* by Shel Silverstein)

Description

This free-verse question-and-answer poem has four couplets. The first line of the couplet asks a question; the second line gives a response. The first two questions begin with "How many...?" and the last two questions ask "How much...?" The answers always begin with "Depends on..." Additionally, the answer to the first question may rhyme with the answer to the second question (rhyming is optional).

Lead-in Activity

Read the two example poems that follow. Ask the students to make note of the question/answer format. Then, on the chalkboard, make two columns: "how many?" and "how much?". Pair the students with a partner and have each pair create one question that begins with "How many...?" and one question that begins with "How much...?" Have them share their questions with the rest of the class, writing their questions under the appropriate column. Ask the students if they can tell the difference between the two types of questions. (Generally, "how many?" questions require a result that can be measured by counting; "how much?" questions require answers that cannot be measured.) Invite students to brainstorm things that cannot be measured (for example, happiness, love, pain, sorrow). Have them write their own poems. Encourage them to use their best ideas from the chalkboard and from brainstorming.

Measurement Poem #1

How many clouds up in the sky?
   Depends on the weather.
How many kids can sit on a couch?
   Depends on how close together.
How much pain in a dentist's chair?
   Depends how long you sit there.
How much good in what you do?
   Depends on nothing else but YOU!

—Roberto, grade 8

Measurement Poem #2

How many angels can fit on a pin?
   Depends on how small, how tiny, how thin.
How many pieces in a pie?
   Depends on how hungry are you and I.
How much noise can one boy make?
   Depends on how much his throat can take.
How much joy is in the sky?
   Depends on where the eagles fly.

—Tannis, grade 7

Social Studies Extension

Obtain a copy of the most recent population census for your country. Ask the students to imagine they have been given the task of counting all the people in North America. Ask them: "How would you do this?" Put students into small share groups and have them formulate a plan that would best enable them to complete this task. Have a spokesperson for each group share the ideas with the rest of the class. Ask the students to articulate what kinds of measurement problems they might encounter (for example, people may not respond or they may have moved away). Encourage interested students to research how real census takers deal with these measurement issues.

Language Arts Extension

Have students select something that cannot be measured (for example, hope or friendship). Ask them to write a short essay that incorporates their reflections on the following questions:

- How can you measure [*student's selection*]?
- How can you know when you have enough [*student's selection*]? Give an example.
- Is it possible to have too much [*student's selection*]? If so, give an example.

Math Extension

Ask the students how they might find out how many students are in the classroom, if they did not know. Explain that counting is a viable way to measure when numbers are small, but it is not always practical. For example, ask students if they know how many square feet (meters) are in their classroom. How would they count them? Explain that there is a way to figure out how many square feet (meters) are in the room without actually counting everything. Show them the formula for finding the area of a square or rectangle (area = length x width). Measure one side of the room if the room is a square and two sides if the room is a rectangle. Help them to compute the area of the room.

 # Plurals

Description

Irregular plurals are the subject of this seven-line poem. The format alternates between a statement about plurals and a question. The poem concludes with a personal observation by the poet. The last word of the question rhymes with the last word of the statement. The poem offers a "what if?" game to readers that results in some ludicrous rhymes.

Lead-in Activity

On the chalkboard or overhead, make two columns. In one column, list words that have regularly formed plurals (for example, boy, girl, table, chair). In the other column, list words that have irregular plurals (for example, calf, goose, mouse, sheep). Start with the words that have regularly formed plurals, and ask for the plural of each word. Ask students what the rule is for forming plurals of such words. Then ask them for the plurals of the words in the second column. Ask the students if there is one rule that governs such words (unfortunately, no!). Encourage students from other language groups to share the difficulty such words caused them when they were first learning to speak English. Finally, read the following poems aloud and brainstorm some other problematic plurals that could be used for new poems.

Plurals #1

The plural of man is men.
  Is the plural of pan then pen?
The plural of goose is geese.
  Is the plural of moose then meese?
The plural of mouse is mice.
  Is the plural of house then hice?
That would be nice!

—Raúl, grade 6

Plurals #2

The plural of that is those.
  Is the plural of rat then rose?
The plural of go is goes.
  Is the plural of no then noes?
The plural of this is these.
  Is the plural of kiss then kese?
Oh, please!

—Rachel, grade 7

Language Arts Extension

Explain to children that in the English language a word that poses a spelling problem because it does not follow the rules is called a "snurk." "Snurk" applies to any word that is not spelled the way it sounds (for example, laugh, the, give). On a sheet of butcher paper, keep a running count of all the words the students notice in the next few days that qualify as "snurk" words. On the final day of this activity, write GHOTI on the chalkboard and ask the students if they know what it says. Explain that, if you spell it with all "snurk" words, it could spell "fish": the "gh" sounds like "f" in the word laugh; the "o" sounds like "i" in the word women; and the "ti" sounds like "sh" in the word nation.

Social Studies Extension

Discuss with students the English language and where it comes from. Show examples of Old English and ask the students if they are able to read it easily. In what ways has it changed? Study regional dialects and compare how different words are used for the same thing in different parts of the country. For example, in some places a round object used for holding water is called a "pail"; in other places it is called a "bucket." Similarly, carbonated beverages are called "pop" in some areas and "soda" in others. Have students make a dictionary of items that have several possible names.

Physical Education Extension

Bring a beachball into the classroom and play a game called "Beachball Plurals." In this game, the leader throws the ball at another person and says a singular word. The person who catches the ball then says the plural of the word, and throws it at another person, saying a new singular word. The game continues until everyone has had a chance to say a singular word and a plural.

# **6** **Tutti-Frutti**

Description

This is a four-line nonsense poem. It combines an enjoyable playing-with-language exercise with a simple rhyme scheme. Even the most reluctant writers will find it irresistable. Because the poem is so playful and unstructured, it is also a wonderful vehicle through which ESL learners can use both their languages.

Lead-in Activity

Introduce students to hyphenated words in the English language (for example, hurdy-gurdy, topsy-turvy, hoity-toity). Have them think of other hyphenated words, and write these on the chalkboard. Ask the students what they think of when they read or hear such words (most find them quite humorous). Put students in small share groups. Ask each group to think up some nonsense rhymes that might go with the hyphenated words they have brainstormed. Tell the students they can create original words if they wish (for example, "hari-kari, where's my teddy *beary*" or "topsy-turvy, you've got some *nervy*!"). Finally, read the example poems and point out the "forced" rhymes. Have the small share groups expand their rhymes into one-stanza poems.

Hurly-Burly (Tutti-Frutti #1)

Hurly-burly, little girly,
A topsy-turvy world this is.
Hunky-dory, what's the story,
Coca-cola with a fizz.

—*Whitney, Jane & Kirsten, grade 5*

Rinky-Dinky (Tutti-Frutti #2)

Rinky-dinky, wash the sinky,
Puppy-doggy goes for a walk.
Hanky-panky, act so swanky,
Mumbo-jumbo is the way I talk.

—*Will, Delon & Geoff, grade 6*

Art/Language Arts Extension

After all the group poems have been edited and final copies have been written, have the students in each group illustrate one line from their poem with colored felt-tip pens. Create a class book of "Tutti-Frutti" poems; put one poem and the corresponding drawing on each page.

Multicultural Extension

Have the students each interview one person they know who is bilingual. Have them ask that person for a list of hyphenated words in his or her home language. Have students share these words, and their meanings, with their classmates. Then, write the words on chart paper. Invite interested students to write cross-cultural "Tutti-Frutti" poems, using words from other languages.

Music Extension

Lead students in a rendition of "Old MacDonald had a Farm," "Purple People Eater," "Mares Eat Oats and Does Eat Oats," or other songs you know that feature language play. Ask the students to bring in songs from home that contain similar fun with language. Have them respond to the following question:

- Why do you think word play is fun for people?
- Do you think people from all language groups like to play with words?
- Why do you think word play makes good poetry?

⑦ Chain of Events

Description

Students enjoy this build-upon format poem. It is concrete and they can visualize every line. The free-verse cumulative format uses seven phrases. The phrases build on one another to show the location or action of one object or animal, and move from large to small, small to large, or person to person, as in the second poem example.

Lead-in Activity

Read the example poems aloud. Ask the students what they notice about what the poem tells them. Then, as a group, have them describe in a similar way the exact location of someone in the classroom (for example, "Jose is in the classroom. The classroom is in the school. The school is in the city. The city is in the state. The state is in the country. The country is in the world. The world is in the universe."). Write the group poem on the chalkboard. Write other examples on the chalkboard, such as "a pair of scissors in a drawer," "a grain of sand in the desert," or "an eyelash on an elephant." Encourage students to think of many examples of cumulative locations using inanimate objects. Finally, have everyone write their own poems using the items they have brainstormed. Pair students for enhanced enjoyment.

Chain of Events #1

The bee is on
The petal is on
The flower is on
The table is on
The floor is on
The building is on
The ground.

—Artur, grade 4

Chain of Events #2

The mosquito is annoying
The baby is annoying
The brother is annoying
The sister is annoying
The father is annoying
The mother is annoying
Me.

—Sonia, grade 5

Art Extension

Have the students, in their original pairs, make a cumulative, flip-up, seven-page book of their poems. In this book each page will be 2" (5 cm) longer than the page before it. Start by giving each pair of students five pieces of 11"x 14" (28 cm x 35.5 cm) white construction paper. To make the first page, have the students cut a piece that is 1/7 the size of a whole sheet (it will be 2" (5 cm) long). On that piece, have them write the first line of their poem. Beside it, have them use colored pencils or markers to draw a picture of the animal or object mentioned in the first line of their poem. For the second page, have them cut a piece that is 2/7 the size of the whole sheet (it will be 4" (10 cm) long). On it, have them write the second line of the poem on the bottom 2" (5 cm) of the piece of paper. (Tell them to always write on the bottom 2" (5 cm) of each page of the flip-up book; see diagram below.) Then, have them draw the animals/objects mentioned in the first and second lines of their poem. Have them continue in this way until all seven items have been completed. Finally, put the pages together to make a book. Start with the smallest piece—the beginning line—on top, and end with the last line of the poem as the last page of the book. Staple the seven pieces at the top, then flip-up as you read the poem.

Language Arts/Art Extension

In this extension, each student has an opportunity to create sentences, sketch, and act out scenes. Tell students they are going to play a game called "What Did Jack Do?" On the chalkboard, write ten prepositional phrases and number them from one to ten (some examples are "on the table," "under the car," "over the haystack"). Divide the class into three groups and number them group #1, group #2, and group #3. Assign each student in the first group a number. Tell this group that you are going to call out two numbers: the first number will be the number of a student in the group and the second number will correspond to one of the prepositional phrases written on the chalkboard. The student whose number you call has to "Tell What Jack Did" by adding a verb to the prepositional phrase (for example, "Jack hid under the car"). Group #2 then draws a quick sketch of Jack hiding under the car, and group #3 acts out the sentence. When all the students in group #1 have added a verb to a prepositional phrase, rotate the groups so everyone gets an opportunity to do everything. This activity can be played over several days.

Music Extension

Share the popular children's song "There Was an Old Woman Who Swallowed a Fly." Ask students what this song has in common with the poems they have just written (they are all cumulative). In their original writing pairs, encourage students to set their poems to music, or rhythmic, rap-like chants. Further, ask them to add actions to accompany their poem/songs; for example, the bee could be represented by a rapid flapping of a finger on each hand; the petal could be shown by pantomiming picking the petals off a daisy. Invite students to perform their new creations for the kindergarten or any group of younger children.

 # Motion Poem

(Adapted from *Seal* by Rachel Field)

Description

In this semi-prescribed poem format, students write a thoughtful description about an animal or mechanical object and how it moves. The format is as follows:

See how he/she [*verb*]—
[*Prepositional phrase*]!
See how he/she [*verb*]—
[*Prepositional phrase*],
Past [*adjective noun(s)*]
And [*adjective noun(s)*]
Past [*adjective noun(s)*]
And [*adjective nouns(s)*]
See how he/she [*verb*]!
With a [*any phrase*]
And a [*any phrase*]
And a [*any phrase*].

Lead-in Activity

Show students a short video (try a five-minute excerpt from a *National Geographic* video) that highlights the movements of a wild animal such as a cheetah, or a graceful bird such as an osprey. Before sharing the video, tell students to pay careful attention to how the animal moves through its environment. Encourage them to think of action words (verbs) that describe the movements of the animals and birds they are watching. After they have viewed the video, write these words on the chalkboard or overhead. Next, read the example poems aloud, and have the students explain what they observe about the structure. Then write a group poem about the animal in the video using the scaffold provided. Finally, invite students to write their own motion poems about their favorite animal or mechanical object.

Kitten (Motion Poem #1)

See how she plays—
   with her catnip mouse on the floor!
See how she leaps—
   through our backyard
   Past flowers and bushes
   And the huge oak tree,
   Past robins and bluejays
   And our German shepherd sound asleep.
See how she relaxes
   With a purring of her motor
   And a twitch of her whiskers
   And a flip of the tip of her tail.
                    —*Vanessa, grade 6*

Camaro (Motion Poem #2)

See how it accelerates—
   from 0-60 in sixteen seconds!
See how it maneuvers—
   through the rush hour traffic
   Past trucks and jeeps
   And bulky RVs
   Past old station wagons
   With screaming kids in the back.
See how it breaks down
   With a sputter and groan
   And a whine of the engine
   And a big sigh from the driver!
                    —*Marc, grade 9*

Science Extension

Invite students to research the animal or mechanical object they have written about in their poem. Have them find out more about how the animal/object moves, what source of energy supports its movement, and how fast it goes. Have the students present their information to the rest of the class. Use a matrix or bar graph to compare the various speeds of the animals or objects. Finally, for those who chose an animal, have them show how that animal's speed helps it survive in its habitat.

Math Extension

Have the students take the information from the chart created in the science activity above, and make up word problems that incorporate the concepts of "faster" and "slower." For example, the cheetah's fastest speed is 80 MPH (128 kmph). How much faster can the Camaro go than the cheetah? How long will it take the cheetah to go 120 miles (192 km)? How long will it take the Camaro to drive the same distance? Encourage students to work out their word problems in small groups.

Art Extension

Ask each student to find a picture of his or her animal or object in motion. Use books, magazines, encyclopedias, and other available resources. Tape a large piece of butcher paper to a wall of the class-room. Have the students paint their animal or object with tempera paints on the butcher paper, using the picture of their animal or object as a guide. Above each portrait, have students write the top speed of their animal/object and any other interesting information they have discovered. Finally, have students attach a final draft of their "Motion Poem" underneath the portrait. Use white paper mounted on a half sheet of colored construction paper.

Someday

(Adapted from *By the Sea* by Adele H. Seronde)

Description

This poem provides a reflective outlet for the poet's longings for faraway places and adventures. The two-stanza, free-verse format, is as follows:

I say
Someday
That I shall [*verb*]
[*Where*],
[*How*],
[*How*].

[*Verb*] [*noun*]
[*How*],
[*How*].
Repeat last three lines of first stanza.

Lead-in Activity

Have students close their eyes while you lead them in a guided imagery of an adventure to a place that has always fascinated them. Choose a foreign country that they have heard a lot about. Help them hear the new language and sounds, see the new sights, feel their heart pounding as they realize a dream and respond to unfamiliar surroundings. When you have finished, ask students to share a place where they have always wanted to travel to. Write the different ideas on the chalkboard and select one to write a group poem about. Read the poems that follow, then invite students to write their own using a similar format.

On the Mountain Top (Someday #1)

I say
Someday
That I shall climb
To the top of Mount Everest,
With the wind in my hair,
And the sun on my face.

Reaching the blue
Of the sky
With my heart.
To the top of Mount Everest,
With the wind in my hair,
And the sun on my face.

—Melissa, grade 9

By the Banks of the River Seine (Someday #2)

I say
Someday
That I shall stroll
On the banks of the River Seine,
Near an outdoor café,
By the light of the moon.

Filling the night with humming
Of no tune in particular,
To everyone I see.
On the banks of the River Seine,
Near an outdoor café,
By the light of the moon.

—Rosco, grade 8

Social Studies Extension

Have students use a world map or globe to find the places they wrote about in their "Someday" poems. Place a colored pin on each location and list them on chart paper. Beside each location include: the country, the latitude and longitude, what the place is known for, approximately how far it is from where you live, the language the people speak, the currency, and other pertinent information.

Art Extension

Have the students use pastels on tag board to create travel posters of the places they long to see. Create a gallery display of the posters. Then, invite the students to give a short talk about the place on their poster using the information they collected in the Social Studies activity (above). Make sure they tell why they would want to go there. Have students conclude their talk by reciting their "Someday" poems.

Math Extension

Give each student two thousand dollars in "play" money. Tell them they are going to plan a one-week journey to their desired destination. Have them consult travel magazines, call airlines and travel agents, contact someone who has been to the location, and create a budget for the trip. Instruct them to include the flight, hotel, food, sightseeing, tips (show them how to figure out 15 percent), ground transportation, and souvenirs. Explain they can spend any excess money on shopping. Have them share their budgets with the rest of the class.

⑩ Matching Poem

Description

This unusual two-stanza poem begins with a common word that can be paired with many other words (for example, gold digger, gold mine, gold rush). After the students each select a word, they think of all the other words that can go with their word. They then place the common word and one of the other words together, creating eight two-word lines, forming a pleasing design. A ninth line consists of a short comment using the word, usually in a humorous vein.

Lead-in Activity

Play "Match Game" with the students. Take a common word that is often paired with other words, such as "heart," "right," "low," "cat," "cold," or "back." Ask the students for words that form a connection with the word. Write their responses on the chalkboard. See how many "matches" they can think of for each word. Then read the following poems aloud. Point out how the ninth line deviates from the other lines in order to make a pithy comment about the subject. Use the ideas on the chalkboard to write a group poem, then read it aloud. Finally, have pairs of students choose a different word and write a poem of their own.

Blue (Matching Poem #1)

Blue moon,
Blue berry,
Blue Boy,
Blue blood.

Blue Cross,
Blue Shield,
Blue grass,
Blue mood.
—Blue hoo!

—Miriam & Alana, grade 5

Cat (Matching Poem #2)

Cat nap,
Cat nip,
Cat's eyes,
Cat's paw.

Cat'o'nine,
Cat kin,
Cat call,
Cat's pajamas.
—Cat got your tongue?

—Craig & Nuri, grade 6

Language Arts Extension

Divide the class into small research groups. Have each group find out the origin of certain expressions that seem somewhat strange to them (for example, "cat's pajamas," "cat got your tongue," or "blue moon"). Invite the groups to share their discoveries with the rest of the class.

Music Extension

The repetition inherent in "Matching Poems" makes them excellent for rap chants. Assign students to their original writing groups, then have them use clapping, finger snapping, and other body movements to turn their poems into rap songs. Optionally, encourage them to use recordings of instrumental music to set the beat for live performances of their renditions before other classes.

Art Extension

Have the students make books. They can use colored markers to create a cartoon for each of their word duos (for example, "cat's pajamas" could be a cartoon of a Garfield-like feline in striped pajamas).

⑪ A Year in the Life

Description

This reflective seven-line, free-verse poem describes one year in the life of the poet. If desired, the poem may include several seven-line stanzas and cover more than one year in the poet's life. The poem adheres to the following format:

When I was [*a specific age in the poet's life*]
I [*what poet did*],
And I [*what else the poet did*],
And I [*what else the poet did*],
And I [*what else the poet did*].
The world was a very [*adjective*] place,
When I was [*age*].

Lead-in Activity

Read A. A. Milne's poem *Now We Are Six*. Ask students what they remember about being six years old. Have them share their reminiscences. Ask them if they can think of a year in their life that was more important to them in some way than their sixth year. Invite them to share, in small groups, the highlights of their most significant year. Read the following poems aloud. Ask the students what they observe about the structure of the poems. Ask them to write a similar poem about a year that was especially significant to them. Tell them that the year needn't have been their best year, as the example poems suggest. It could be their most successful year, their most eventful year, their most memorable year, and so on.

A Year in the Life #1

When I was seven
I went to a new school,
And my parents got a divorce,
And I lost all my old friends and had to make new ones,
And I felt shy about all these changes.
The world was very undependable,
When I was seven.

—Dustin, grade 4

A Year in the Life #2

When I was five
I still believed in Santa Claus,
And I thought the tooth fairy put money under my pillow,
And I believed the Easter Bunny brought me candy,
And I believed everything my parents told me.
The world was a fairy tale,
When I was five.

—Emily, grade 4

Art Extension

Discuss the word *perspective* and how our perspective changes as we grow and learn. Explain, also, that in art the word is used to convey a person's way of seeing an object or a landscape, depending on the angle and the distance it is seen from. Demonstrate by showing how a chair looks entirely different sideways, from a bird's-eye view, and from below it. Have students select one of these ways to look at a chair, then draw it from that perspective. Have them share their drawings and then make statements about what perspective means to them.

Science Extension

Assign pairs of students to do a science experiment with kinder-garten-age children. Arrange with the kindergarten teacher for his or her students to meet with your students for about ten minutes. Give each pair of your students two tumblers: one tall and thin and the other short and wide. Instruct your students to tell the younger child to watch as water is poured from the short, wide tumbler into the tall, thin tumbler. Then instruct the pair to ask the young child: "Which glass has more water in it?" Because young children have not had enough experience with this concept, they will invariably say the taller tumbler contains more water. Back with the whole class, have the pairs of students share their findings with everyone. Ask them to make statements about the differences in perspective between themselves and the kindergarten children.

Social Studies Extension

Show students an example of a historical time line. Give them some twine or clothesline. Have them stretch their own time lines across the room. Fasten the ends at opposite walls of the classroom. Ask them to then think about specific milestones in their lives, and write a brief paragraph describing each on 5" x 8" (13 cm x 20 cm) cards. Invite the students to date each milestone and attach it at the appro-priate place on their time lines.

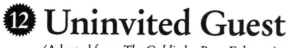 Uninvited Guest

(Adapted from *The Goblin* by Rose Fyleman)

Description

This tongue-in-cheek prescribed poem concerns an uninvited "guest" that lives with the poet. The first two and the last two lines are identical. The middle of the poem contains four pairs of rhyming couplets that describe the actions of the guest. The scaffold looks like this:

A [*name of guest*] lives in/on *my* [*location*], *my* [*location*], *my* [*location*],
A [*subject*] lives in/on *my* [*location*], all [*time period*] long.

He/She [*verb*],
And he/she [*verb*],
And he/she [*verb*],
And he/she [*verb*].

He/She [*verb*],
And he/she [*verb*],
And he/she [*verb*],
And he/she [*verb*].

A [*name of guest*] lives in/on *my* [*location*], *my* [*location*], *my* [*location*],
A [*subject*] lives in/on *my* [*location*], all [*time period*] long.

Lead-in Activity

Ask students if they have ever had an imaginary friend. Have them share these experiences. Then ask them if they have ever had an "uninvited" guest, such as a mouse or a pesky fly, in their house. After reviewing the definition of verbs, or action words, have students brainstorm some words that tell why the "guest" was not wanted. Write their words on the chalkboard. Ask the students to tell how long their guests stayed with them and how they finally got rid of them. Finally, read the example poems aloud. Write a class group poem, using the poem format and the students' brainstormed ideas. Then, ask the students to write their own poems.

The Spider (Uninvited Guest #1)

A spider lives in *my* room, *my* room, *my* room,
A spider lives in *my* room all day long.

She wiggles,
And she jiggles,
And she grins,
And she spins.

She hides,
And she rides,
And she scurries,
And she hurries.

A spider lives in *my* room, *my* room, *my* room,
A spider lives in *my* room all day long.

—*Sandrine, grade 5*

The Rabbit (Uninvited Guest #2)

A rabbit lives in *our* garden, *our* garden, *our* garden,
A rabbit lives in *our* garden all summer long.

He hops,
And he stops,
And he itches,
And he twitches.

He munches,
And he lunches,
And he runs,
And he suns.

A rabbit lives in *our* garden, *our* garden, *our* garden,
A rabbit lives in *our* garden all summer long.

—*Bethan, grade 4*

Art Extension

Distribute sheets of white paper, black construction paper, white chalk, and colored markers to each student. Ask the students to use the chalk to draw the place (room, house, garage, and so on) where their live-in guests reside (use a chalk-setting spray to keep the pictures from smudging). Then, on the white paper, have each student draw the guest mentioned in their poem, engaged in one of its activities, and color it using colored markers. Have them cut out the "unwanted guest" and glue it onto the black-and-white chalk-drawing. Decorate the classroom with the drawings, and place the students' final drafts of their poems underneath.

Language Arts Extension

Invite students to recite their poems using audience participation. Ask the poet to recite the first two lines and the last two lines alone. Then assign (or allow the poet to assign) a different child to recite each of the rhyming couplets. They might want someone with a high voice to say the light or happy couplets and someone with a lower voice to recite the "moodier" couplets.

Science Extension

Ask the students to define the word *pest*. Do they consider spiders to be pests? Rabbits? Mice? Why or why not? Make a list of the creatures they consider pests. Discuss each and explain when each actually is a help to farmers or has other uses in the food chain.

 Admiration Poem

(Adapted from *Trees* by Harry Behn)

Description

This poem is a kind of eulogy to an animal, object, or group of people. The format is as follows:

[*Subject*] are the [*adjective*] [*what they are*] I know.
They [*what they do*],
And they [*what they do*],
And they [*what they do*].
They [*what they do*],
And they [*what they do*],
And they [*what they do*].
But mostly because they [*what they do*]—
[*Subject*] are the [*adjective*] [*what they are*] I know.

Lead-in Activity

Harry Behn, the author of *Trees*, writes: "Trees are the kindest things I know." Ask students why the poet might feel that way. Ask them to share what they might describe as the kindest things (not people) they know. Next, have them share the "coolest machines" they know, and ask them to explain why. Then read them the example poem *Motorcycles* aloud. Ask them to share what they would consider the "finest animals" they know and tell why. Follow this discussion by reading the example poem *Dogs* aloud. Invite them to create an original "Admiration Poem," using the prescribed format and some of the ideas they have shared.

Motorcycles (Admiration Poem #1)

Motorcycles are the coolest machines I know.
They make lots of noise when you rev the engine,
And the handlebars turn and twist under your hands,
And you feel strong and powerful riding them.
They take you anywhere you want to go,
And they go much faster than a bicycle,
And they give you a better view than being in a car.
But mostly because they are exciting to ride on—
Motorcycles are the coolest machines I know.

—Jamal, grade 9

Dogs (Admiration Poem #2)

Dogs are the finest animals I know.
They look up at you with big adoring eyes,
And they wag their tails every time they see you,
And they will follow you anywhere you go.
They know when you're in a bad mood,
And they try to make you feel better,
And they will never leave your side.
But mostly because they will love you no matter what—
Dogs are the finest animals I know.

—Shayna, grade 6

Language Arts Extension

After the students have completed their poems about animals, machines, and other non-humans they admire, ask them to think about what person in their life they most admire. Allow them to select small share groups in which to discuss the person they most admire and their reasons. Back in the whole group, ask the students if they have ever told their chosen person how they feel. Ask them how they feel such a compliment might be received. Then, provide attractive stationery and encourage the students to write a letter to their chosen person, explaining why they feel the way they do.

Art Extension

Invite students to make the final drafts of their "Admiration Poems" on plain white paper, then adhere each to colored construction paper shaped like the animal or object that is the object of their admiration. Mount the poems on a bulletin board labeled "We Admire..."

Social Studies/Math Extension

Have pairs of students select a grade and specific class from your school. Ask them to survey the children in their chosen class to determine each child's most admired person. When the students are finished with this assignment, chart the results according to age and gender of respondents. Further classify the most admired people according to their occupation. Ask students to make any concluding statements they can from the results, such as "more fifth-grade girls than boys greatly admire presidents (or prime ministers)" or "More third-graders than second-graders named sports figures as their most admired people."

 Month Madness

Description

This twelve-line poem is a spoof on the abbreviations of the months of the year. The first line begins with "If your life began in..." and ends with an abbreviation of a month. Subsequent lines provide an internal rhyming pattern. The poem begins with any month the poet wishes, usually the poet's birth month. The sentiments expressed can be as zany as desired.

Lead-in Activity

Read students the humorous story *Chicken Soup with Rice* by Maurice Sendak (see page 117, appendix A for more information). Ask them what is special about this book (each page concerns a month of the year). With the students, chorally recite the names of the months of the year in order. Ask them for the abbreviation for each month and write them on the chalkboard. Tell students they are going to write some very unusual calendar poems using these abbreviations. Read the example poems aloud. Finally, put the students in groups of three and encourage each group to write its own "Month Madness" poem.

March Baby (Month Madness #1)

If your life began in Mar., you will break a jelly jar.
You'll inhale water vapor in Apr.,
And go far away in May.
You'll eat with a spoon in June,
And jump in a pool in Jul.
You'll catch a frog in Aug.,
And lose a pet you kept in Sept.
You'll open the door you locked in Oct.,
And eat a bread loave in Nov.
You'll hunt for geese in Dec.,
Get a dark tan in Jan.,
And spin a spider's web in Feb!

—*Jared, LeToya & Crystal, grade 5*

New Year's Baby (Month Madness #2)

If your life began in Jan.,
You'll find a friend named Jeb in Feb.
You will not travel far in Mar.,
But your name will be in the paper in Apr.
You'll stub your toe one day in May,
And sing a sorry tune in June.
You'll ride a little mule in Jul.,
And ride a big fat hog in Aug.
To town you will have crept in Sept.,
And gossip will make you shocked in Oct.,
You'll sail a boat into a cove in Nov.,
So you're tired, to say the least, in Dec.!

—*Katherine, Henryk & David, grade 6*

Science Extension

Have the students create a science calendar. Divide the class into groups and have each group research different scientists (for example, Marie Curie, Louis Pasteur, Luther Burbank, Charles Darwin). Provide a time for them to share the information they discover with the rest of the class. On each month's page on the calendar, assign a student to draw a picture of one of the scientists and provide interesting facts about his or her work. Have other students compose mini-biographies of the lives of the scientists and put these below the pictures.

Art Extension

Have students paint a mural depicting the various months of the year, using butcher paper and tempera paint. Assign two or three students to a month and ask each group to consider what clothing would be worn that month in the climate in which you live. Select an activity described in the "Month Madness" poems and ask members of each group to paint portraits of themselves engaged in that activity, dressed in the appropriate seasonal clothing for the month. When the mural is finished, arrange the final drafts of the students' poems around the perimeter of the butcher paper.

Math/Social Studies Extension

Have the students use a comprehensive atlas or other resource to compare the temperatures in various cities around the world during various months of the year. Find the cities on a map or globe. Ask students what differences they notice between cities south of the equator and cities north of the equator. For example, places south of the equator have summer when we have our winter. Ask them to hypothesize why they think this is so. Finally, invite the students to create number sentences using the symbols for greater than (>) and less than (<) to make up number statements comparing the average temperatures in various cities around the world.

 Count-Down Poem

(Adapted from *Five Little Butterflies*)

Description

This ten-line poem describes the gradual departure of people or animals, from five to none. Couplets may be rhymed with a number, but rhyming is optional. The format is as follows:

Five [*adjective*] [*subject*] [*verb*],
One [*verb*] and then there were four.
Four [*adjective*] [*subject*] [*verb*],
One [*verb*] and then there were three.
Three [*adjective*] [*subject*] [*verb*],
One [*verb*] and then there were two.
Two [*adjective*] [*subject*] [*verb*],
One [*verb*] and then there was one.
One [*adjective*] [*subject*] [*verb*],
[*Concluding phrase*].

Lead-in Activity

Have students close their eyes while you read the poem *Five Little Butterflies* aloud to them (see page 117, appendix A for more information). Ask them to imagine how the last butterfly is feeling as all her friends fly away. Afterwards, have the students share their images in small share groups. Read the example poems aloud and ask the students to explain how these poems are similar to the first poem you read. Ask the students what animals or imaginary people they would like to write about. Invite them write their own poems. Have them use structure in the example poems, or copy the above structure on the chalkboard for them to use as a guide.

Five Lonely Bandits (Count-Down Poem #1)

Five lonely bandits running out the door,
    One had a heart attack; then there were four.
Four lonely bandits hiding behind a tree,
    One ran off to rob a bank; then there were three.
Three lonely bandits paddling a canoe,
    One fell overboard; then there were two.
Two lonely bandits always on the run,
    One got arrested; then there was one.
One lonely bandit getting tired of all the crime,
Gets a wife and finds a job; now he's happy all the time.

—*Eduardo, grade 6*

Five Baby Bunnies (Count-Down Poem #2)

Five baby bunnies hopping on a field,
    One went in a hole; then there were four.
Four baby bunnies twitching their pink noses,
    One goes off to find some food; then there are three.
Three baby bunnies hiding in the bushes,
    One falls asleep in the sun; then there are two.
Two baby bunnies looking for a home,
    One gets chased by a fox; then there is one.
One baby bunny not knowing what to do,
I hope he finds his mother before the day is through!

—*Cole, grade 5*

Language Arts Extension

Have students find pictures representing each character in their poems. They can use magazine pictures or free-form drawings. Have them paste these pictures or drawings onto lightweight tagboard and cut them out. Then have them unfold paper clips and tape them to the bottom of each of the cut-out characters. Now the students will have a "shadow puppet" they can use with the overhead projector as they recite their poems. Invite them to present a shadow puppet recital with their puppets and their poems. (Note: This is a terrific Parents' Night activity.)

Science Extension

Discuss with students the survival alternatives of "fight or flight." Revisit their poems to determine which creatures fought and which creatures simply ran away when they were in a threatening situation. Ask the students to think of a time when they were in a "fight or flight" situation. Invite them to share what they did and what the outcome was. Finally, ask them if they think they would react differently today.

Math/Social Studies Extension

Discuss the concept of "ordinal" numbers with the students. Then, have them talk about the subject of their poems using the ordinal numbers from one to five (for example, "The first baby bunny didn't know what to do..."). Next, show them how the early Romans made their numbers. Write the Roman numerals one to five on the chalkboard. Finally, invite students who speak a second language to share the numbers one to five in their home languages. Encourage those who are interested to rewrite their "Count-Down Poems" using Roman numerals or numbers from another classmate's language.

Warning Poem

(Adapted from *If You Should Ever Meet a Crocodile* by Sara and John Brewton)

Description

This six-line poem contains three rhymed couplets, offering the reader dire warnings about the consequences of doing certain deeds. The start of each couplet begins with the words, "If you should ever..." Poets may concentrate their efforts on true-to-life dangers, such as drinking alcohol, or more whimsical pastimes, such as chasing tigers.

Lead-in Activity

Ask students to tell about some activity they have been repeatedly warned not to engage in. Encourage them to share who has warned them and why they think they are being told not to pursue the activity. Ask them about something they did that caused them harm. What warnings would they give to others so that they wouldn't do the same thing? Have them brainstorm warnings they could give about imaginary things no one would ever do (for example, swallow a canary, sneak up on a gorilla). Read students the poem *If You Should Ever Meet a Crocodile* by Sara and John Brewton (see page 117, appendix A for more information), or the poem *Warning* by Shel Silverstein. Ask students why they think the poets chose the subjects they did. Finally, show them the example poems and point out the specific format. Invite them to use ideas from the preceding discussion, or others, to create their own poems about real or imaginary dangers.

Warning Poem #1

If you should ever meet a whale
Never hold it by the tail.
If you should ever meet a goat
Don't put a collar around its throat.
If you should ever meet a boy
Never use him as a toy!

—Sasha, grade 4

Warning Poem #2

If you should ever start to smoke
You will hack and cough and choke.
If you should ever tell a lie
You'll get found out by and by.
If you should ever say a word that's bad
You'll have to answer to your dad!

—Paul, grade 4

Art Extension

Give the students large pieces of construction paper and colored markers, and ask them to make posters illustrating the warnings in their poems. Around the real or imagined dangerous activity, have them draw, in red markers, a circle and a diagonal line going through it. Encourage them to read their poems while holding up their posters and pointing to the illustrated idea for emphasis.

Language Arts/Science Extension

Discuss with students some of the warnings they may have heard that are really only superstitions. Some examples are: if you break a mirror you will have seven years of bad luck; if a black cat crosses your path you will have bad luck. Make a list of all the superstitions the students can think of. Then, ask them to select one, research its origin, and try to "debunk" it, or scientifically explain why it could not be true.

Health/Art Extension

Invite a nurse or other health care professional into your classroom to speak to the students about things they should and should not do to lead a healthy lifestyle. Beforehand, have the students discuss and write down several questions about health that they would like to have answered. After the presentation, divide the class into small groups, and have each group write and illustrate a brief handbook for others, featuring "the top ten ways to be healthy."

 # Five Words

Description

In this free-verse poem, students think of their favorite words and reflect on important feelings they have about them. Each of the five lines contains a favorite word and what that word means to the poet. Putting these feelings into words makes interesting, yet easy-to-write poetry.

Lead-in Activity

Tell students you are going to take away all the words in the world except five. Ask them which five words they would most like to keep. The words can be feeling words, names, expressions, or even nonsense words. Have the students share their favorite words in small groups, explaining why each word is special to them and their reasons for keeping it. Then, ask each student to write a short phrase next to each word telling why it is important. This creates a lovely and reflective poem.

Shalom (Five Words #1)

Daddy—you are everything to me;
Holiday—vacations and a break from school;
Fear—my favorite emotion to feel during a scary movie;
Whatever—when you just don't know what to say;
And...shalom—peace and hello and goodbye!

—Lisa, grade 4

Taco (Five Words #2)

Love—let's keep it in the world;
Excellent—tops! the best! Truly fine!
Bummer—how else do you describe a bad day?
Taco—awesome taste, funny word;
And...friend—so loyal, so there for me, so YOU!

—Michelle, grade 7

Language Arts Extension

Take the lead-in activity one step further. Ask students to imagine that, suddenly, there are no words in the world. Discuss how life as we know it would be different without language. Ask the students to brainstorm some ways they might communicate without any spoken or written language. Make a list of all gestures they know that are used in place of spoken language (for example, the "high five" sign, the "victory" sign, the "okay" sign). Introduce the students to the finger spellings and some simple signs from American Sign Language (ASL). Invite them to practice sending simple messages to each other using this form of communication.

Social Studies Extension

Ask children to keep a "values notebook." In it, they will create a page for each item/idea/belief that they hold dear. For each value, have them find a picture from a magazine or draw a picture to represent that value. Underneath each picture, have them to write a brief explanation of how the picture stands for their value. Encourage children to select their "top five" values and pictures to share with other children in small share groups.

Art Extension

Ask students to bring in old magazines from home. Encourage them to look through the magazines for pictures that represent each of the five words they used in their "Five Words" poem. Have them carefully tear out these pictures. Next, give them sheets of colored construction paper. On this paper have them glue their pictures to make a colorful collage of their five words. In the center of the collage, have them glue a final draft of their "Five Words" poem written on a half sheet of plain white paper. Use these collages to create a delightful bulletin board highlighting the students' favorite words.

# New Wisdom

Description

This easy-to-write poem has no set number of lines. It requires students to use their imagination—and a bit of common sense—to create new endings for traditional adages. Every line begins with the first few words of the original adage and the rest is completed by the poet. The result is fresh and delightful poetry.

Lead-in Activity

Define the word *adage*. Then, write several adages on the chalk-board (for example, "You can lead a horse to water, but you can't make him drink," "People who live in glass houses shouldn't throw stones"). Discuss what these adages mean. Ask students why they think people continue to use these phrases instead of communicating the idea more directly. Explain that you are going to pass out a list of adages, but the endings will be missing. Tell the students you want them to think of imaginative endings for the adages. When they are finished, have them select their best phrases and arrange them in a pleasing design.

New Wisdom #1

All work and no play...
   Is a boring life!
A rolling stone...
   Is a very old rock group!
All that glitters...
   Usually costs too much!
You can't teach an old dog...
   How to shake hands!
Don't count your chickens...
   While they are in the frying pan!

   —Alison, grade 4

New Wisdom #2

A penny saved is...
   Not very much money.
A bird in the hand...
   Should be allowed to go free.
A man and his money...
   Should go to the bank right away.
Water seeks its own...
   Ocean, lake or pond.
When at first you don't succeed...
   Try another way to do it.

   —Mario, grade 4

Social Studies/Art Extension

Have students ask people they know from other countries about adages, or sayings, in their home language. Instruct the students to ask the people to write down the adage in their home language and also to write out the translation. Back in the classroom, invite students to share the adages they discovered. Discuss if any are similar to any that they know in English. Make a multicultural class book that includes the newly found adages in the original language, the translation of the adages, and the country from which each comes. Finally, have interested students illustrate the adages using watercolors.

Language Arts Extension

Read several of Aesop's Fables aloud. Tell the students to pay close attention to the moral of each story. Invite them to write their own short stories based on one of the original adages they have learned. Have them read their finished stories to the rest of the class.

Music Extension

Have the students sing a traditional folk song such as "On Top of Old Smokey" or "You Are My Sunshine." Tell them that they are going to write their own song to the tune of the song they have just sung. Have small groups compose short musical ballads around the theme of the adage of their choice. Have them share their ballads with the rest of their classmates and, if desired, students in other classes.

⑲ Nonsense Poem

Description

This simple four-line verse has two (sometimes three) words per line and consists of an animal or other item and the sound it makes. The last line is a nonsense phrase that can be easily made to rhyme with the last word in the second line. Students can create as many stanzas as they wish.

Lead-in Activity

Discuss the word *onomatopoeia*. Young students find this concept fascinating—especially when the sounds come from animals (for example, dog: bow-wow) or from a familiar everyday item (for example, car: beep beep). On the chalkboard, write a list of animals in one column. Next to this column ask students to tell you the sound associated with this animal. Have them help you sound out the spelling of the word. Then, write a list of common items students are familiar with (for example, clock, bell, fountain, saw). Ask them what sounds they associate with these items. Again, have them help you sound out the spelling of these words. Then, ask students to think of nonsense rhymes to go with the sounds (for example, moo moo—boo hoo; ding dong—can't go wrong). Read the example poems aloud to show how others have used nonsense rhymes to make playful poetry. Finally, after writing a group poem using the items and sounds listed on the chalkboard, have pairs of students write their own poem.

Nonsense Poem #1

Slam, door!
Rub-a-dub, tub!
Beat, heart—
Blub, blub!

Tick, clock!
Buzz, bee!
Purr, cat—
Tee hee hee!

Neigh, horse!
Zoom, car!
Honk, horn—
Har de har!

—Dean & Glen, grade 6

Nonsense Poem #2

Bang, drum!
Baa, sheep!
Goo goo, baby—
Go to sleep!

Slam, door!
Ring, phone!
Scream, little boy—
Ice cream cone!

Roar, engine!
Chirp, cricket!
Crack, bat—
Sticky wicket!

—Len & Thomas, grade 6

Language Arts Extension

Read the students a short story that contains many sounds (a ghost story or Hallowe'en story is good). Provide the appropriate sound effects for the story. Distribute cards containing words that could be substituted for the sounds (for example, buzz, creak, thud, groan). Reread the story. Choose students to hold up the sound card at the appropriate time in the story. Read the story a third time; this time have the rest of the students provide the sound effects by reading the card as it is held up. Ask students which way they prefer the story to be read.

Social Studies Extension

Have students interview adults they know in the community who are bilingual. Instruct them to show their poems to the person they have selected and ask that person to share in their home language how the animal or object in the poem says its sound. (Note: Students will be interested to find out that animal sounds vary from language to language; for example, in English, a rooster says "cock-a-doodle-doo"; in Spanish, it says "corro-clo-clo.") When the students have finished their interviews, have them share what they have learned with the rest of their classmates. Make a class pamphlet showing how animal sounds vary in different languages.

Music Extension

Borrow a metronome from the music teacher. Ask students to read their poems to a slow beat. Invite others to clap along with the beat, creating a rap-like chant. Finally, encourage the students to move their bodies to the rhythm in dance-like motions. Using this method, chant everyone's poem, one after the other. Ask students if such an activity adds to the enjoyment of the poems.

# Participle Poem

Description

In this two-stanza, eight-line poem, the poet uses participles (verbs as nouns) to talk about his or her favorite activities. The format is as follows:

[*Participle*] is [*description*],
[*Participle*] is [*description*],
[*Participle*] is [*description*],
[*Rhyme with line two*].

[*Participle*] is [*description*],
[*Participle*] is [*description*],
I'd [*comment on topic participle*]
If only I [*rhyme with line two*].

Lead-in Activity

Ask students to share their favorite activities (for example, skiing, hiking, reading, drawing). Write the responses on the chalkboard. Ask them to tell you what they observe about the names of all the activities listed on the chalkboard (the words all end in "ing"). Explain that when an action word, or verb, is used as a noun it is called a "participle" and always has an "ing" on the end. Invite children to create sentences using participles at the beginning (for example, "Skiing is best when the day is sunny and bright"). Read the example poems aloud, asking the students to pay careful attention to the structure. Encourage them to write a poem featuring their favorite— or least favorite—activity.

Swimming (Participle Poem #1)

Swimming is soggy
Floating's a chore,
Wading is wet,
I'll stay on the shore.

Diving is scary,
Treading water is slow,
I'd rather live in a desert
If only I could go!

—*Sergei, grade 8*

Having Fun (Participle Poem #2)

Playing is pleasing,
Talking's a treat,
Phoning is fabulous,
Napping is neat.

Laughing is lovely,
Giggling is good,
I'd spend my life happy
If only I could!

—*Joanna, grade 9*

Drama/Language Arts Extension

After the students have written their poems, initiate a guessing game. Have the students, one at a time, act out the subject of their poem using a modified Charades format: After the activity being acted out is guessed, have the student read his or her poem aloud. Then, have the student read the poem a second time while the rest of the class joins in the charade.

Music Extension

Encourage students to set their poems to music, using a simple tune such as "Twinkle, Twinkle Little Star." When each song is set to music, encourage trios of students to go to the classrooms of younger children. There, they can introduce their poems with song and, using the actions devised in the drama extension, invite the audience to participate in both the singing and the acting.

Math Extension

On chart paper, list the favorite activities of all the students in the class. Using a simple bar graph, compare the interests of the boys and the girls in the class. Are there major differences? Are students surprised by the findings? Discuss why this may or may not be so. Have students calculate the percentage of people favoring each activity. Finally, follow the same procedure for the students' least favorite activities.

㉑ Peace Poem

Description

Every line in this free-verse poem begins with either "Peace is…" or "Peace is not…" The lines may alternate between a description of what peace is and a description of what peace is not. There are no set number of lines.

Lead-in Activity

Have students close their eyes and think of a place that makes them feel very peaceful. Ask them to think of what it is about the place that makes it seem so peaceful. Distribute 3" x 5" (7.5 cm x 13 cm) cards to the students and ask them to write down where their favorite peaceful place is. Collect the cards and redistribute the cards. Have the students go around the classroom and find the person whose card they now have by asking: "Is your most peaceful place to be _____?" When they find the owner of the card, have them spend a few moments sharing their feelings with the other person about their peaceful place. Next, read the following poems aloud. Then, invite students to write their own poems.

Peace Poem #1

Peace is having the bathroom all to myself;
Peace is NOT when my brother tries to knock down the door!
Peace is sitting in the backyard watching the starry night;
Peace is NOT when the sky is full of pollution!
Peace is having a great happy dream;
Peace is NOT when I have a terrible nightmare!
Peace is the country and wide open spaces;
Peace is NOT the city with the traffic and the noise!

—*Carla, grade 5*

Peace Poem #2

Peace is NOT people arguing and fighting—
Peace is my family and friends all getting along.
Peace is NOT the bumper cars—
Peace is a gentle Ferris wheel ride.
Peace is NOT a ferocious thunderstorm—
Peace is a warm spring rain.
Peace is NOT an angry lecture by a red-faced parent—
Peace is a smile and a pat on the back.

—*Oksana, grade 5*

Social Studies Extension

Provide materials about the following peacemakers:

Jimmy Carter	Lester B. Pearson
Mahatma Gandhi	Sacajawea
Golda Meir	Martin Luther King, Jr.

Divide the class into small groups and have each group answer the following questions about a peacemaker. Students can research one of the above peacemakers or select someone currently in the news.

• What did the person do to gain the reputation as a peacemaker?
• What should we all know about your peacemaker's life?
• How did your peacemaker believe conflicts should be settled?

Invite the groups to share their information with the rest of their classmates.

Language Arts/Social Studies Extension

Explain to the students that conflict in itself is not "bad"; it is the way that conflict is handled that determines if peace will continue. Ask small groups to role-play the following scenarios. Have the rest of the students watch and reflect on how the situation could be handled peacefully.

- A student takes a pencil from another student's desk without asking.
- Three children want to play with the same ball at recess.
- A child trips another child while they are waiting in line.
- The boys won't let the girls play basketball with them.

Art Extension

Have students create a bulletin board divided into two parts. The top part will have blue butcher paper, with fleecy white clouds made with shredded cotton. The bottom half will consist of grey or black butcher paper, to represent storm clouds or the dark of night. Instruct students to write the lines from their poems on narrow one-inch (2.5 cm) strips of white construction paper. Invite them to then place their "Peace is..." statements on the top, blue sky section of the bulletin board, and the "Peace is not..." statements on the lower, stormy part of the bulletin board.

# You're Special

(Adapted from *That's Amy* by Marci Ridlon)

Description

This poem promotes self-esteem and helps people learn to appreciate one another. The poem has two stanzas, each containing two rhyming couplets. The format is as follows:

What makes [*student's name*] [*verb*] so [*adverb*]?
[*Description of prowess*].
[*Description of prowess*],
[*Description of prowess*].
—That's [*student's name*]!

Repeat.

Lead-in Activity

Write the name of each student in your class on separate 3" x 5" (7.5 cm x 13 cm) cards. Shuffle the cards and distribute them, one to each student. Take care not to give any student his or her own card. Then ask the students to think of something that the person on their card does really well. (Warn them not to write put-downs. What they write must be "true" and "good" and should concern a quality or talent, rather than a physical attribute.) When everyone is finished, collect the cards, briefly review them, and put them aside. Read the following poems aloud. Be sure to point out the structure and rhyme scheme. Select several of the cards and have the students write group poems, using qualities contained on the cards. Finally, pair the students and invite each to write a "You're Special" poem about the other.

You're Special #1

What makes Belinda draw so well?
She does portraits that are really swell.
She makes things look just like they should,
I've never seen anyone draw as good.
—That's Belinda!

What makes Belinda draw so well?
How she does it she'll never tell.
She always has a pencil and pad,
You should see how she can draw her dad.
—That's Belinda!

—Sylvana, grade 4

You're Special #2

What makes Bradley know so much?
He knows all about the world and such.
He's as smart as the best machine,
He gets the best grades I've ever seen.
—That's Bradley!

What makes Bradley know so much?
God must have given him a special touch.
He always has an intelligent plan,
And explains so even I can understand.
—That's Bradley!

—Christopher, grade 6

Language Arts Extension

At a special time, have students gather in a circle in their chairs or on the floor. Ask one student to read his or her poem aloud to the person he or she has written about. Encourage everyone else to add to that student's good qualities or talents by offering a statement beginning with: "I appreciate [*student's name*] because he/she [*description*]." Ask the student being talked about to reply, simply, "Thank you!" Go around the circle in this manner until everyone's poem has been read and everyone has been in the spotlight.

Social Studies Extension

Ask the students how they felt in the previous activity when people were noticing each other's best qualities. Discuss how the world could be a kinder place if we all concentrated on each other's best qualities—and ignored the worst! Ask the students to keep a log for one week of the kind words or deeds they say or do with their family, friends, and classmates. At the end of the week, have everyone share the results of their positive words and deeds.

Science Extension

Explain the word *unique* to the students. Ask them what they think makes them unique. On the chalkboard, list as many traits as every-one can think of that are unique to only one child in the classroom. Then, find a diagram of a DNA strand (try a science textbook or CD-ROM). Explain to the students that this tiny strand is in each of us. It contains all the information that makes us who we are. It's what make us each different from every other human.

 **Congratulations**

(Adapted from *The Swan*)

Description

This poem is used to congratulate an animal on its successful round-trip journey to anywhere in the poet's imagination. Alliteration, gentle word play, and the present, past, and past perfect tenses of a verb are used to make this four-line, free-verse poem delightful to students. The format is as follows:

[*Animal*] [*past tense verb*] [*prepositional phrase*]—
[*Command*], [*animal*], [*command*];
[*Animal*] [*past tense verb*] back home again,
Well [*past perfect tense verb*], [*animal*]!

Lead-in Activity

Read *The Swan* to the students (see page 117, appendix A for more information). Ask them to "echo" each line after you. The alliteration makes it fun to read aloud. Read the two example poems in the same manner. Then, ask the students to brainstorm other animals that they could write about. (Note: Animals with names beginning with consonant blends or digraphs, such as chickadee, squirrel, shark, and crawdad work best.) For each animal that has been brainstormed, have students think of an action word that begins with the same beginning sound (for example, "crawdad crawled," "scorpion scooted"). Finally, using the brainstormed ideas and the poetry scaffold provided, encourage students to write their own "Congratulations" poems.

The Flamingo (Congratulations #1)

Flamingo flew across the lake—
Fly, flamingo, fly;
Flamingo flew back home again,
Well flown, Flamingo!

—David, grade 7

The Snake (Congratulations #2)

Snake snuck through the grass—
Sneak, snake, sneak;
Snake snuck back home again,
Well snuck, snake!

—Ali, grade 8

Language Arts Extension

Discuss regular verbs (for example, help, reach, want) and how their present, past, and past perfect tenses are formed. Discuss irregular verbs and how to form past tenses with them (for example, swim, fly, drive, sneak). Provide a sentence to help the students remember how each tense is used; for example, present tense: "Today I drive a jeep." Past tense: "Yesterday I drove a jeep." Past perfect tense: "I have driven a jeep." Have the students brainstorm some actions or gimmicks they could use to help them remember which tense is which. For example, they could use these signals:

• index finger pointed down: "Today I..." (present tense)
• one thumb pointed behind: "Yesterday I..." (past tense)
• arms across chest with both thumbs pointed backwards across shoulders: "In the past I..." (past perfect tense)

Science/Art Extension

Discuss how animals in the wilderness use camouflage to protect themselves from predators. Have the students find out if the animal in their "Congratulations" poem camouflages itself for protection. If so, how? Finally, have the students draw a picture of their animal in its natural habitat, showing how it uses camouflage. Have them read their poems while holding up the picture of the animal.

Physical Education Extension

Playing Charades is another way students can share their poems. Have them write the names of their animals in their poems on 3" x 5" (7.5 cm x 13 cm) cards. Then, have them take turns randomly selecting a card and reading aloud the name of the animal. The poet recites the poem and another student acts out the animal's movements. Play until everyone has had a chance to read his or her poem.

 Career Poem

(Adapted from *Busy Carpenters* by James S. Tippett)

Description

This is a three-stanza poem that extols the virtues of a particular career or trade. In it, the poet muses about the tools of that career or trade. The brief verses follow this format:

The song of the [*tool used in the job*]
Is [*adjective describing the tool*]
As they [*action of the tool*]
[*Rhyme with line two*].

Repeat twice.

Lead-in Activity

Bring a hammer, saw, or plane to the classroom and ask the students what each is used for. Ask them if they know anyone who is a carpenter or someone who has made something out of wood. Ask them: "What is special about making something with your own hands?" "Why would a carpenter have a special feeling about these tools?" Then, read the example poems aloud and ask them the same questions about people who choose these occupations. Have the students brainstorm other occupations and write these in one column on the chalkboard. In another column, write ideas the students have about what "tools" might go with each occupation (and therefore might be special to one who does this work). Invite students to write their own poems.

The Farmer (Career Poem #1)

The song of the pitchfork
Is fine
As they get the hay in
Just barely in time.

The song of the reaper
Is grand
As they grow food to eat
From the rich land.

The song of the tractor
Is loyal
As they plow the fields
And till the soil.

—Sabrina, grade 7

Fire Fighter (Career Poem #2)

The song of the fire truck
Is speed
As they rush to the fire
And help people in need.

The song of the water hose
Is kind
As they put out the flames
And save people they find.

The song of the siren
Is caring
As they spend their whole lives
Doing deeds that are daring.

—Jim, grade 8

Language Arts Extension

Divide the class into small groups. Ask the students to share with their group what they want to be when they grow up. Invite them to write a short essay addressing the following questions:

- Why do you want to be a _____ ?
- Who is a model for you in this career?
- Describe what you think a day in your life might be like when you have become a _____ .

Social Studies Extension

Hold a Career Week in your classroom. After sharing students' essays, have each student find an adult who is doing what he or she wants to do. Provide the students with questions they can ask that person. Some examples are: "When did you first become interested in becoming a _____ ?" "What is the best thing, in your opinion, about being a _____ ?" If you want, have the students solicit the address and telephone number of the person so you may invite them into the classroom to give a five-minute overview about their occupation. Alternatively, have students present the results of their interview to the rest of their classmates.

Art Extension

Have the students look through magazines for a picture of someone doing what they want to do. Or, have them create their own sketch. Mount the pictures in the center of a bulletin board labeled "Our Career Goals." Attach everyone's "Career Poem" around the periphery of the board.

⑳ Synesthesia Poem

Description

In this free-verse format, poets think of a common object they usually associate with one particular sense, and perceive it through an entirely different sense. There are no set number of lines. The format is as follows:

[*Subject*] [*sense*] _____ .
No one ever _____ .
It's always _____ .
But [*subject*] [*sense*] _____ .

Lead-in Activity

List the five senses (sight, hearing, smell, taste, and touch) on the chalkboard or overhead. Ask students to brainstorm some examples of things they usually experience through only one sense (for example, a painting is usually seen; a salad is usually tasted; perfume is usually smelled; Plasticine is usually felt). Ask students to think of some zany alternative ways they might experience these items. Show them the scaffold above and have them choose one item from their list to describe in this different way (for example, they are going to tell what the painting might smell like; what the salad might feel like; what the perfume might sound like, and so on). Read the following poems aloud to further illustrate the creative possibilities. Then invite students to write their own poems. Tell them they can use ideas that have been listed or they can use their own ideas.

A Star (Synesthesia Poem #1)

A star feels like glass,
Smooth, hard, and fragile.
No one ever thinks to touch it.
It's always just 'look at that.'
But stars are lonely,
Smooth, hard, and fragile.

—*Emma, grade 8*

A Chair (Synesthesia Poem #2)

A chair sounds quite unhappy,
Especially when it is being squished by people.
No one ever hears it groan and moan.
It's always very quiet when people are around,
But it would complain LOUDLY
If you bothered to ask it, "How are you?"

—*Alexei, grade 9*

Art Extension

Write the word *anthropomorphism* on the chalkboard. Explain that this very large word is used when human characteristics are assigned to animals or objects (which is what happened in the above poems). Tell the students they are going to take this concept one step further by making a cartoon figure of the object of their poem. Then, have them give the figure a mouth with a balloon coming out of it for a caption. Instruct them to make the caption from the most important idea in their poem. Have them attach their poem underneath the cartoon. Collect all the cartoons and poems, and make them into a class book.

Language Arts Extension

Ask the students which sense they feel is the most important. Have them write an essay on that sense. Ask them to outline "a day in the life" and describe how they use that sense on an hourly basis. Have them share their essays with the rest of their classmates. Finally, tally which sense the majority of the students consider most important.

Science Extension

Distribute balloons to all the students in the classroom and help them to blow them up and tie them. Put students in groups of five and assign a particular sense to each person in the group. Then ask the students to experiment with their balloons and come up with five phrases describing their balloons, one for each of the five senses; for example, "Our balloon feels as soft as satiny skin," or "Our balloon smells like stale bubble gum." Invite the students to share their phrases by asking all who were assigned the sense of smell, for example, to share the phrases their group decided on. Write all the phrases on the chalkboard under the appropriate sense.

Intonation Poem

Description

In this unusual free-verse poem, students find out how emphasis on certain words affects the meaning of the entire sentence. The poem format consists of the same sentence repeated five times. Each time, the emphasis is placed on a different word, and is followed by a parenthetical comment on the meaning of the sentence. A final phrase offers the reader a personal comment about the content of the poem.

Lead-in Activity

Ask students to listen carefully as you clearly read the sentence: "I drove to the circus yesterday." The first time you read the sentence, emphasize the word "I." The second time, emphasize the word "drove." The third time, emphasize the word "circus," and the fourth time emphasize the word "yesterday." Each time you read the sentence, ask the students what they think you mean. For example, when you say, "I *drove* to the circus yesterday," you probably mean you could have walked or ridden your bicycle but, for some reason, you chose to drive there instead. Discuss the meaning of each sentence. Then read the example poems aloud. Be sure to point out how the poets' comments and final phrase make interesting poetry. Invite small groups of children to write their own poems.

The Story (Intonation Poem #1)

That is the best story I've ever written.
(Not *this* one; *that* one.)
That *is* the best story I've ever written.
(Don't you be doubting it; it's true!)
That is the *best* story I've ever written.
(It's definitely not the worst.)
That is the best story *I've* ever written.
(But *you've* written some good ones.)
That is the best story I've ever *written*—
But I've *told* some better ones!

—*Rayleen, Matthew & Tyler, grade 8*

Rollerblade (Intonation Poem #2)

I finally learned how to Rollerblade.
(You've been doing it for years.)
I *finally* learned how to Rollerblade.
(It's taken me FOREVER.)
I finally *learned* how to Rollerblade.
(Now I really know how to do it.)
I finally learned *how* to Rollerblade.
(I was doing it, but not right.)
I finally learned how to *Rollerblade*—
But not how to stop when I'm going 90 miles an hour!

—*Owen, Marette & Dylan, grade 7*

Language Arts Extension

Divide the class into small groups of four or five students. Have each group write a short, humorous skit about the confusions that can result when we use the wrong intonation when giving information or instructions (tell the students they can use some of the ideas in their "Intonation Poem"). Invite the groups to share their skits with the class.

Art Extension

Assign the students to their original writing groups, then ask them to each select a line from their poem and illustrate how the context changes when the emphasis changes; for example, in *Rollerblade*, the first line might show a boy triumphantly taking his first strides on his Rollerblades as some friends, ahead and in a pack, look back, notice, and gesture for him to join them; the last line might feature the same boy running into a tree because he is not able to stop.

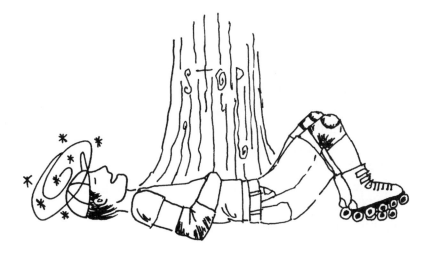

Social Studies Extension

After writing their poems, students begin to see how important intonation is in the English language. Bring in information about other languages in which intonation is even more important. For example, in Mandarin the pitch of the voice, whether rising or falling at the ends of words, creates totally different word meanings. If possible, invite a speaker of an Asian language to come into your classroom and demonstrate the importance of intonation, then have the visitor teach the students some simple words and phrases in his or her language.

 # I Dream

Description

In this free-verse poem, every line begins with "I dream..." There are no set number of lines. You can add game-like rules (for example, each line must contain a color, an emotion, a book character, a food) if you want.

Lead-in Activity

The week before you introduce this poem idea, ask the students to keep a detailed log of all the dreams they can remember. Invite them to share their favorites—the most interesting, the zaniest, the most realistic, and so on. Discuss with them the nature of dreams: they can be unfulfilled fantasies or embody what we are most afraid of, but often dreams are whimsical and, therefore, can make good poetry. Read the example "I Dream" poems aloud and point out the simple structure. Have the students use their dream logs to contribute ideas for a group poem, with or without "rules." Read the group poem chorally and then ask the students to write their own "I Dream" poems.

I Dream #1

(rules: use a color and an emotion)

I dream I am running into an emerald green forest and
   bloodhounds are chasing me so I am very afraid;
I dream I have on a red velvet dress and I keep hoping
   Jared will notice me;
I dream I am sailing on a crystal blue lake and I feel
   at peace with the world;
I dream my newly permed brown hair catches fire and
   I am terrified I am going to die;
And I dream I am a queen and I am so proud of the way all
   the people are green with envy whenever they look at me.

—Lauren, grade 7

I Dream #2

(rules: use an emotion and a color)

I dream a bomb explodes in the black night and all the people
   are frightened and they're hoping I will save them;
I dream I am galloping on a brown pony and the pony and I
   are feeling as free as the wind;
I dream I am flying in the blue sky but I am petrified I might fall;
I dream I am wearing my blue cowboy shirt to Grandma's and
   somehow she gets mud all over it and I am ashamed;
I dream I am in a rodeo and I am nervous because I am being
   asked to ride the black, evil-looking bull;
And I dream I am very rich and all this green money comes
   raining down on me.
How do you think I feel??? Delirious!

—Andy, grade 6

Science/Health Extension

Divide the class into three groups. Have each group focus on one of the following questions: "What are dreams?" "Why do we dream?" "What is REM sleep?" Have the groups share their findings with the rest of their classmates. Follow these presentations with a discussion about how much sleep the students get compared to how much sleep children their age need. Have them share how they feel when they have been sleep-deprived for a number of days.

Art/Language Arts Extension

Ask the students to write "tall tale" stories in the first person. Tell them to exaggerate an event that actually happened to them, or to make up a story (for example, they meet a famous basketball player who plays one-on-one with them; they dig a deep hole and find a colony of strange talking animals). Encourage them to end their preposterous story with an "easy out": "I woke up. It was all a dream." Invite them to colorfully illustrate their "tall tales."

Social Studies Extension

Ask the students to do a survey of the sleeping and dreaming behavior of the students in your school. Assign each student a grade and class. Have them ask the following questions, then record the results:

• Do you ever dream in color?
• How many dreams do you usually remember in a night?
• Have you ever dreamed you were flying?
• How much sleep do you get every night? (What time do you usually go to bed and rise in the morning?)

When all the surveys have been completed, discuss the results, chart them, and publish them in the school newspaper.

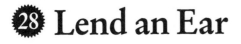

28 Lend an Ear

Description

Poets begin this free-verse poem by telling where they are. Then they describe what they can hear from this vantage point. The description should be so vivid that the reader could guess the location without having it verbally identified. The name of the location is repeated at the beginning and at the end of the poem.

Lead-in Activity

Ask the students to think of quiet places (for example, a library, by a lake) and noisy places (for example, a playground, an airport, a midway). Write their responses on the chalkboard in one column labeled "places." Label another column "sounds." Ask the students to brainstorm sounds they might hear if they were to sit very quietly and listen in each of the places mentioned in the first column. Ask them if they would be able to tell where they were just by listening in these places. Read the example "Lend an Ear" poems aloud and ask the students to note how the poets use vivid auditory descriptions to show us rather than tell us where they are. Invite students to write their own "Lend an Ear" poems. They can use the brainstormed places and sounds, or they can use ones they think of.

In the Park (Lend an Ear #1)

Sitting in the park I hear
The sounds of children laughing,
And birds chirping and singing sweet songs.
I hear squirrels chattering to one another
And the wind rustling through the trees.
And I hear a quarrel between a teenager and a younger kid,
And a mother's angry voice as she tries to quiet them.
I hear the whoosh of a swing, a squeal of delight,
and the steady squeak of a teeter-totter.
Sitting in the park I hear the sounds of my neighborhood.

—Alicia, grade 8

From My Bed (Lend an Ear #2)

Lying in my bed I hear
The sound of my dad snoring,
And my little brother Pierre mumbling in his sleep.
I hear the house creaking, making me just a little scared;
And I hear a dog barking outside,
Making me wonder what he is hearing.
I hear a car door slam from down in the street,
And some teenagers talking loudly and cursing
As they walk toward their house.
Lying in my bed I hear the sounds of the night—
And I'm glad I am not alone.

—Robyn, grade 8

Language Arts Extension

Take the students to a park near your school. Ask them to sit still for five minutes and, in a notebook, record every sound they hear. Tell them to try not to look around to identify the sound. Discuss their findings, and ask them what they learned about their sense of hearing from the exercise.

Social Studies Extension

Ask the students to imagine they have lost their sense of hearing. Discuss how their daily routine would change with such a loss. Then, as an assignment, have them watch a cartoon on television with the volume turned off. Ask them to pay particular attention to the cues they use to figure out what is going on. Back in the classroom, have them share their observations with the rest of their classmates. Finally, teach them the finger spelling symbols for sign language and a few basic signs (books containing helpful diagrams are available in the public library). Discuss these symbols as a viable means of communication.

Science Extension

Show students the components of the human ear (use a large three-dimensional model, CD-ROM, or other resources) and explain how sound waves work (they travel in differing frequencies, which allows us to hear the vibrations as sound). Have the students experiment with different pitches. Make rough sketches on the chalkboard or overhead to illustrate what is happening.

 # I Wonder

Description

In this speculation poem, poets ask all those questions that have always intrigued them. The poem begins with "I wonder..." There are no set number of lines and rhyming is optional.

Lead-in Activity

Ask students if they have ever wondered about something for which they have never received a satisfactory answer. For example, have they ever wondered why we can't see wind? What makes the light in a firefly? Why do flowers come in so many different colors? Have students sit in a circle on the floor. Invite them to share some things they have always wondered about. Have them start their statement with "I wonder why/how/where..." Then read the example poems aloud. Divide the class into groups of three and have each group write a poem, using ideas from the discussion that they have brainstormed in their small group.

I Wonder #1

I wonder why a dog comes when you call and a cat doesn't;
I wonder why, when you look at your reflection in a spoon,
   it's upside down;
I wonder why ice melts and glass doesn't;
I wonder why the burners on the stove are red when they're hot;
I wonder why we get sick;
I wonder why we have to sleep;
I wonder why birds can fly and we can't;
I wonder where butterflies go in the winter;
And I wonder who I'll marry!

—*Celine, Vicki & Jennifer, grade 5*

I Wonder #2

I wonder why a boat floats;
I wonder how dogs know how to swim when no one teaches them;
I wonder why we have tears when we cry;
I wonder what makes a rainbow;
I wonder why you can see your breath when it's cold;
I wonder why lightening never strikes the same thing twice;
I wonder how stars twinkle;
And I wonder how the world began.

—Eddie, Jess & Vladimir, grade 6

Social Studies Extension

Ask students if they have ever wondered about the customs of people from other countries (for example, taking off one's shoes to enter a house in Japan; eating with chopsticks in many Asian countries). Ask them to imagine they are coming to this country for the first time. You could also ask students who are immigrants to share any customs they found strange when they arrived here (shaking hands; throwing rice at the bride after a wedding). Divide the class into small share groups. Have the students imagine how they would explain a custom to someone just arriving in North America. When everyone is back in the large group, point out that customs from other countries only seem "strange" because we are unfamiliar with them.

Science Extension

Select many of the "I wonder..." statements from the students' poems and present the scientific explanations for them (this could actually dictate your science curriculum for most of the year!). Revisit the poems at a later date. Decide which questions can be/or have been answered (for example, "What makes a rainbow?") and which will probably never be answered (for example, "Why does a dog, but not a cat, come when you call it?").

Language Arts Extension

Have students select an "I wonder..." statement about why things are the way they are (for example, "Why do birds fly when we can't?" "Why do we have to sleep?"). Have them brainstorm some advantages and some disadvantages if the situations were reversed (for example, what might be the advantages of people being able to fly? What might be some disadvantages?) Then, ask students to write a three-paragraph essay stating the advantages, the disadvantages, and, finally, which situation they think they would prefer.

# Jump Rope

Description
This rhythmic poem borrows its structure from the sing-song chants many children recite when they jump rope. The poem consists of three simple rhyming couplets addressed to some animal or object.

Lead-in Activity
Ask students to chant with you as you recite the familiar jump-rope rhyme that follows:

Teddy bear, teddy bear, turn around,
Teddy bear, teddy bear, touch the ground.

Teddy bear, teddy bear, go up stairs,
Teddy bear, teddy bear, say your prayers.

Teddy bear, teddy bear, turn out the light,
Teddy bear, teddy bear, say good night!
—*Traditional*

Have students share other jump-rope rhymes they know. Ask them to reflect on why they think these rhymes have been handed down from generation to generation, and what is special about them. Read the following poems aloud and point out how these have captured the sing-song flavor of the "teddy bear" rhyme. Finally, brainstorm some subjects that might have the same three syllable cadence as these poems do (for example, "puppy dog, puppy dog"; "hoppy toad, hoppy toad"), and encourage students to write their own poems.

Chickadee (Jump Rope #1)

Chickadee, chickadee, take a bath,
Chickadee, chickadee, make a splash.

Chickadee, chickadee, greet the day,
Chickadee, chickadee, fly away.

Chickadee, chickadee, sing a tune,
Chickadee, chickadee, come back soon!

—Devon, grade 4

Kitty Cat (Jump Rope #2)

Kitty cat, kitty cat, climb a tree,
Kitty cat, kitty cat, chase a bee.

Kitty cat, kitty cat, stalk your prey,
Kitty cat, kitty cat, run away.

Kitty cat, kitty cat, lick your fur,
Kitty cat, kitty cat, purr, purr, purr!

—Kristi, grade 4

Art/Language Arts Extension

Help students make puppets of the subject of their poems. They can use old socks, buttons, crayons, and fabric remnants. Provide a copy of all the poems to the students, or write them on overheads for all to see. Ask the poet to lead the rest of the class in a sing-song rendition of his or her poem. At the same time, have the poet use the puppet to act out the action described in the poem.

Physical Education Extension

Bring students out to the playground. Make sure they have copies of all the class poems. Select two children to swing a jump rope and ask the others, one at a time, to jump to the rhythm of the new "Jump Rope" poems as the rest of the students chant them.

Social Studies Extension

Research if children from other countries use jump ropes in their playground games. Try to find several jump-rope rhymes translated from other languages, and teach them to the students. Or, you may want to ask guest speakers from other countries to come in and teach jump-rope rhymes in their home language. Incorporate these rhymes and the children's poems into a class book of jump-rope rhymes. Some students may want to share a reading from them with younger children in other classes.

⊛ 31 Until

Description

This free-verse, three-stanza poem format describes the first time the poet saw a memorable landmark, natural disaster, or other things in nature. The first two stanzas describe what the landmark does, while the last stanza tells how the viewer feels about seeing it. The format is as follows:

Until I saw [*landmark*]
I did not know that _____ .
Or that _____ .

I never knew that _____ .
Or that _____ .

Nor did I know before that _____ .
Or that _____ .
Until I saw [*landmark*].

Lead-in Activity

Ask students to raise their hands if they have ever seen or been to one of the following: a well-known park such as the Grand Canyon, Yosemite National Park, Banff National Park; natural landmarks such as the Rocky Mountains, the Badlands, Old Faithful, Niagara Falls; historical monuments such as the Statue of Liberty or the Liberty Bell. Ask them: "Was this experience different from what you expected?" "How was it different?" "Were your feelings about what you saw different from what you thought they would be?" "How were they different?" "Why do you think you were surprised?" "Was seeing the real thing better or worse than you thought it would be?" "In what way(s)?" Encourage the students to listen for the ways in which the authors of the "Until" poems learned something interesting about the subject they chose. Have students write their own "Until" poems. Tell them to describe their feelings about a place they have been to, or a place they haven't been to but would like to visit.

The Statue of Liberty (Until #1)

Until I saw the Statue of Liberty
I did not know that so many people longed to come to America.
Or that this great lady was the very first sight they saw.

I never knew that the Statue was so huge that you
would need to take a long elevator ride to get to the top.
Or that you could actually stand in her brilliant tiara.

Nor did I know before that I could feel such pride in my country.
Or that burning tears would suddenly well up in my eyes.
Until I saw the Statue of Liberty.

—Luke, grade 6

Niagara Falls (Until #2)

Until I saw Niagara Falls
I did not know that water could be so loud and frightening.
Or that it could even have the power to make electricity.

I never knew that millions of people a year
would come from every country to hear the pounding water.
Or that they would feel the spray of the Falls from a mile away.

Nor did I know before that I would feel so full of awe.
Or that I would remember that roar forever.
Until I saw Niagara Falls.

—Hannah, grade 7

Social Studies Extension

Place students into small interest groups according to the subject they have selected for their poems. Encourage them to use encyclopedias, CD-ROMs, and other resources to find out as much as they can about the place. Suggest they write to the Chamber of Commerce or tourist bureau and request pamphlets and brochures about the area. Finally, have them incorporate the information they gather into a travel packet that urges others to visit the sight.

Math Extension

Have groups of students calculate approximately how far away their place is from where they live. You can probably find this information in maps and atlases. Have the groups find out how much it would cost to travel to their destination by the various modes of transportation (economy). Finally, have them determine how much it would cost a family of four to visit the site and stay for two nights and three days. Have them calculate their estimates on a per diem for hotels, or campgrounds, and meals at moderately priced restaurants. Have students add this information to their travel packets.

Art Extension

Give the students large pieces of poster board and pastels. Tell them they are going to make colorful travel posters of their chosen place from the information they collected for the social studies activity. At the bottom of their posters have them append their poems. Encourage them to share their posters and informational packets with the rest of their classmates. (Note: You can also use this activity as an open-house project for parents and other classes.)

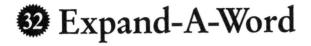

㉜ Expand-A-Word

Description

In this prescribed, five-line, free-verse poem, poets name a favorite item. They then describe and re-name the item, tell where it might be found, how it can be used and, finally, how they feel about the item. The format is as follows:

First Line: [*Name of item*].
Second Line: [*Describe and rename item*],
Third Line: [*Where item can be found*],
Fourth Line: [*What can be done with the item*],
Fifth Line: [*How the poet feels about the item*].

Lead-in Activity

Tell students to imagine an English-speaking alien is visiting the classroom and trying to find out as much as possible about life in North America. Have them brainstorm some of their favorite toys or other items. List these on the chalkboard. Then, ask the students how they might explain to the visitor what each item is, how it is used, and what it means to them, without actually naming the item. Next, pair the students and have each pair act out what they might say to the alien about one of the brainstormed items. Finally, read the "Expand-A-Word" poems aloud. Ask the students if they think the alien would be able to understand the nature of the object through the poets' descriptions.

Lilac (Expand-A-Word #1)

Lilac.
Beautiful lavender flower,
Decorating backyards and gardens once a year,
Filling our kitchen with the scent of early spring,
Seeing you, I feel certain that summer will come.

—Daria, grade 7

Bicycle (Expand-A-Word #2)

Bicycle.
Sturdy, metallic mode of transportation,
Found in a dusty back corner of my garage,
With your help, I can almost fly,
With you, I feel free of the cares of the world.

—Bryan, grade 7

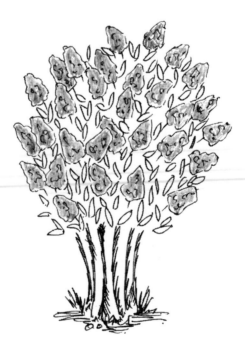

Language Arts Extension

Invite the students to read only the last four lines of their poems to their classmates. Have the other students guess what the item is. Whoever guesses correctly gets to read his or her poem aloud.

Social Studies Extension

After the students have shared their poems, tell them they are going to rewrite their poems. They are going to keep the same idea, but use a different language. As a homework assignment, encourage each child to pair up with someone who is bilingual (this person may be a classmate, a student from another class, a teacher, a relative, a neighbor, or a friend). Instruct the child to have the partner translate the poem into his or her home language, and to explain a bit about his or her language. Encourage the child to memorize how to pronounce the words in the translated poem. Back in the classroom, invite students to recite their poems to their classmates in the "new" language. Then, have them offer the English translation of their poem. Have each child tell what language their poem has been translated into, as well as anything they discovered about the other language.

Art Extension

Give each student a piece of white paper and a pencil. Invite them, one at a time, to come to the front of the classroom and carefully describe an object without mentioning the name of that object. Have the other students draw the object they think is being described. When the drawings are complete, have the child in front reveal the object he or she has just described. Discuss how the description might have been clearer and therefore easier to draw.

 # Let's Go!

(Adapted from the song "A Hunting We Will Go")

Description

This five-line, loosely rhyming poem is borrowed from the folk song "A Hunting We Will Go." In the poem, the poet tells about a favorite activity. The poem can be recited or sung to the original tune. The format is as follows:

Oh, a [*participle—favorite activity*] we will go,
A [*participle*] we will go,
We'll _____ _____ _____ ,
And _____ _____ _____ [*rhymes with above line*]
And then we'll _____ _____ _____ !

Lead-in Activity

With the students, sing the song "A Hunting We Will Go." Ask them if they or anyone they know has ever gone hunting. Then, ask them what activities they have been involved in that they like to do. Point out the "ing" of the word "hunting" and ask them to offer their activities in this "ing" format (for example, fishing, camping, hiking). List their responses on the chalkboard. With the students, write a group song, using one of their suggestions and the blank scaffold above. Finally, read the "Let's Go!" poems aloud. Allow students to put them to music.

A Skiing We Will Go (Let's Go! #1)

Oh, a skiing we will go,
A skiing we will go,
We'll ski down the hill,
And get a big thrill—
We love the powdery snow.

—*Sam, grade 4*

A Shopping We Will Go (Let's Go! #2)

Oh, a shopping we will go,
A shopping we will go,
The neat clothes at the mall,
We'll buy them all—
And then we'll put on a fashion show.

—*Yola, grade 5*

Language Arts Extension

Have students share their poems. Then, have them write a "how-to" paragraph describing the best way to perform their chosen activity. Explain that these paragraphs can be serious or "tongue-in-cheek," providing a humorous look at the activity. After peer-group editing of the paragraphs, create a classroom bulletin board entitled "Our Favorite Activities." Include both the narrative paragraph and the poem each student has written.

Physical Education/Drama Extension

Divide the class into small groups. Within each group, have the children determine a favorite sport's activity. Then have them research (a) how many calories a person would burn doing this activity and (b) the health benefits that may result from the activity. Have each group present its sport in pantomime. Let the other students guess the activity. When the activity has been guessed, have one child from the group (a) write the sports activity on the chalkboard, (b) tell how many calories per hour are burned while participating in this sport, and (c) discuss other physical benefits that can be obtained from the sport. When all groups have presented their sport, make a class booklet about all the sports and the health benefits that can be derived from each activity.

Social Studies Extension

Have the students research the history of the sport they selected. Encourage them to use encyclopedias, CD-ROMs, trade books, and other resource materials. Ask them to pay close attention to:

- the country where the sport originated
- how long the sport has been played
- how the sport has grown in popularity and/or changed over the years

Have students write a paragraph outlining what they have learned about their sport. At the bottom of the paper, have them draw a pen-and-ink sketch of themselves participating in the sport.

 Mood Poem

Description

This poetry scaffold provides an outlet for the intimate thoughts of the more mature poet. The scaffold includes nine lines of free verse, six of them prepositional phrases. The format is as follows:

[Prepositional phrase] ————————— ,
[Prepositional phrase] ————————— ,
I examine ————————————— .
[Prepositional phrase] ————————— ,
[Prepositional phrase] ————————— ,
I begin to ———————————— .
[Prepositional phrase] ————————— ,
[Prepositional phrase] ————————— ,
I welcome ————————————— .

Lead-in Activity

Ask students if they have ever been in a bad mood and why they feel that particular mood may have occurred. Have them think of all the possible moods people can have and how they tend to behave in each of them. Write their answers on the chalkboard. Then, introduce and give examples of prepositional phrases that might be associated with the moods you have brainstormed (for example, "with a happy heart" would go with a joyous mood; "under a black cloud" might be associated with a sad or depressed mood). Share with students the above scaffold, and allow them to examine it as you read the following poems aloud. Ask them how the prepositional phrases used by the poets help to capture each poet's mood. Invite them to write their own "Mood Poem," using the scaffold.

Anger and Healing (Mood Poem #1)

Through my tears,
Amidst overpowering sadness and grief,
I examine my feelings of anger.
During a sleepless night,
With a blanket pulled up around my neck,
I begin to understand my hurt feelings.
With new insights and inner peace,
Under the illusions of a new day,
I welcome the sensation of healing.

—*Anthony, grade 9*

Tired and Broke (Mood Poem #2)

With a bunch of money in my pocket,
From my babysitting jobs,
I examine the cute clothes in the stores in the mall.
As the sun goes down,
With the purchase of everything I could find,
I begin to get very tired, and quite ornery, and my feet hurt.
After I arrive home,
At the end of an exhausting shopping spree,
I welcome the chance to sit and rest.

—*Sara, grade 8*

Art/Language Arts Extension

After students have written their poems, encourage them to share with a trusted friend who can serve as a peer editor. Instruct the peer editors to tell the poet what they like about the poem and to suggest ways to make it even better (for example, by using more evocative words to describe the mood). Have each student make a final copy on a word processor, if available. The poet may also use a computer graphics program or fine-tipped colored markers to create a decorative border that complements the mood of the poem.

Social Studies Extension

Have a discussion about the impact of one's moods on others. Demonstrate this idea by dropping a stone in a pan of water or by drawing ripples on the chalkboard. Compare each individual's own universe to the ripples in the pan. Explain that that person is in the center. Everyone else (for example, classmates) is a ripple around him or her. Outside the classroom are the people in the school itself. Outside that is family, then the community. Show the impact of the ripple on the people in the city or town, state or province, country, continent, world, and even the universe. Ask students to consider creating some guidelines for dealing with moods in positive, rather than negative, ways.

Music Extension

Select five diverse classical music pieces from your own collection (or you might want to check the media center or local library for suggestions). Offer some interesting background information about the first selection and its composer. Then ask students to close their eyes, and while they are listening to the music, think of words, phrases, or impressions that the music brings to mind. When the music has finished, ask them to share their ideas. Write these ideas on the chalkboard. Repeat this process with each of the five selections. After you have played all five pieces, ask the students to consider the poems they have written and decide which of the musical selections would best enhance their poem. Hold a poetry reading for parents or other classes where students read their poems accompanied by the music they have selected from the classical pieces.

 Treasure Walk

(Adapted from *One Day When We Went Walking* by Valerie Valine-Hobbs)

Description

This unusual, two-stanza, eight-line poem has a simple rhyme scheme. Poets can use it to tell about an item they have discovered that turns out to be something other than what it first appeared to be. The poem format is as follows:

One day when I went [*participle*],
I found a/an [*object*]—
A/An [*adjective*] [*object*].
"A/An [*what the object really was*]!" said [*person**].

Repeat.

*(person should rhyme with the object)

Lead-in Activity

Write the word *imagination* on the chalkboard. Ask the students if any adult has ever said to them: "That's just your imagination!" Ask them what they think it means to have a vivid imagination. Is it a good or a bad thing? Tell them that you are going to read them two poems written by poets who were on a walk; their imaginations let them see things in a very special way. After reading the following "Treasure Walk" poems aloud, invite the students to close their eyes. Tell them they are walking in the forest and when they look down they find something. Have them visualize what they might see that might appear to be something else.

Treasure Walk #1

One day when we went hiking,
I found a dinosaur print—
A gigantic dinosaur's print.
"A pothole!" murmured Clint.

One day when we went hiking,
I found a silver key—
An ancient silver key.
"A soda pop tab!" laughed Bree.

—*Juanita, grade 4*

Treasure Walk #2

One day when we went bike riding,
I found a flying saucer—
A mysterious flying saucer.
"It's just a Frisbee!" said Chaucer.

One day when we went bike riding,
I found an antique doll—
A precious antique doll.
"An old beat-up Barbie," giggled Molly.

—*Chrissy, grade 4*

Reading/Listening Extension

Ask the students if they ever lie back on the grass and watch the clouds. Were the clouds shaped like an animal, a person, or some recognizable object? Read students the book *It Looks Like Spilt Milk* by Charles Shaw (see page 117, appendix A for more information). This picture book is full of colorful "blobs" of color that look like different things to different people. Go through the book page by page and ask the students what each colorful form looks like to them. Then, read them the accompanying text to reveal what the author finds in the shapes.

Science Extension

Arrange a "treasure walk" field trip to the nearest park, forest, or wilderness area. Have each student bring a spiral-bound notebook and a pencil. Ask them to carefully observe their environment. Then, have them write down or draw pictures of everything they see that is unusual, that they have never seen before, or that is of particular interest to them. Have them also keep an eye out for "treasures" like the ones the poets found in the "Treasure Walk" poems. Back in the classroom, divide the class into small cooperative groups. Within each group, invite students to read their descriptions or share their pictures and "treasures."

Art/Language Arts Extension

This is a very messy activity, so be sure to line the floor or table tops with newspapers before you begin. Then, give each child a large sheet of construction paper and two tablespoons of tempera paint (any color). Ask students to place the paint in the center of their paper and then fold the paper in two, making a large "ink blot" drawing. In pairs, have the students discuss what the ink blots remind them of. Finally, encourage everyone to write a paragraph telling a story about his or her object.

Appendix A:
Original Poems for Modeling

Behn, Harry. "Trees" in *The Little Hill*. New York: Harcourt, Brace & World, 1949.

Bidlon, Marci. "That's Amy" in *Knock at a Star: A Child's Introduction to Poetry*. Compiled by X. J. Kennedy and Dorothy M. Kennedy. Boston: Little, Brown, 1982.

Brewton, Sara, and John Brewton. "If You Should Ever Meet a Crocodile" in *My Tang's Tungled and Other Ridiculous Situations*. New York: Crowell, 1973.

Field, Rachel. "Something Told the Wild Geese" in *Poems*. New York: The Macmillan Co., 1930.

———. "Seal" in *Poems*. New York: The MacMillan Co., 1930.

"Five Little Butterflies" in *The Random House Book of Poetry for Children*. New York: Random House, 1983.

Fyleman, Rose. "The Goblin" in *Preposterous: Poems of Youth*. Selected by Paul B. Janezko. New York: Orchard Books, 1991.

Merriam, Eve. "Umbilical" in *Quiet, Please!* New York: Simon & Schuster, 1993.

Milne, A. A. "Now We Are Six" in *When We Were Very Young*. New York: Dutton, 1961.

"Mockingbird" in *The Random House Book of Poetry for Children*. New York: Random House, 1983.

Sendak, Maurice. *Chicken Soup with Rice: A Book of Months*. New York: Harper & Row, 1962.

Seronde, Adele. "By the Sea" in *Knock at a Star: A Child's Introduction to Poetry*. Compiled by X. J. Kennedy and Dorothy M. Kennedy. Boston: Little, Brown, 1982.

Shaw, Charles. *It Looks Like Spilt Milk*. New York: Harper & Row, 1947.

Silverstein, Shel. "How Many? How Much?" in *Where the Sidewalk Ends*. New York: Harper & Row, 1974.

"The Swan" in *Preposterous: Poems of Youth*. Selected by Paul B. Janezko. New York: Orchard Books, 1991.

Tippett, James S. "Busy Carpenters" in *The Random House Book of Poetry for Children*. New York: Random House, 1983.

Valine-Hobbs, Valerie. "One Day When We Went Walking" in *The Random House Book of Poetry for Children*. New York: Random House, 1983.

Appendix B:
Suggested Reading

Adults

Ada, A. F., V. J. Harris, and L.B. Hopkins. *A Chorus of Cultures Poetry Anthology: Developing Literacy Through Multicultural Poetry*. Carmel, CA: Hampton Brown, 1993.

Andrews, R. *The Problem with Poetry*. Bristol, PA: Taylor & Francis, 1991.

Armour, M. W. *Poetry, the Magic Language: Children Learn to Read & Write It*. Englewood, CO: Teachers Ideas Press, 1994.

Bauer, C. F. *The Poetry Break: An Annotated Anthology with Ideas for Introducing Poetry to Children*. Bronx, NY: H. W. Wilson, 1995.

Bunchman, J., and S. B. Briggs. *Pictures & Poetry: Activities for Creating*. Worcester, MA: Davis Publications, 1994.

Carroll, J. A. *Poetry Books: Reading, Writing, Listening, Speaking, Viewing & Thinking*. Englewood, CO: Teachers Ideas Press, 1994.

Chatton, B. *Using Poetry Across the Curriculum: A Whole Language Approach*. Phoenix, AZ: Oryx Press, 1993.

Collom, J., and S. Noethe. *Poetry Everywhere: Teaching Poetry Writing in School & in the Community*. New York: Teachers & Writers Collaborative, 1994.

Cullinan, B., M. Scala, and V. Schroder. *Three Voices: An Invitation to Poetry Across the Curriculum*. York, ME: Stenhouse Publishers, 1995.

Garaway, M. K. *The Teddy Bear Number Book: A Bilingual Book (Los Numeros con los Ositos)*. Translated by M. R. Cartes. Tucson, AZ: Old Hogan Publishing, 1995.

Goldish, M. *Thematic Poems, Songs & Fingerplays*. New York: Scholastic, 1994.

Graves, D. *Explore Poetry*. Portsmouth, NH: Heinemann, 1995.

Grossman, F. *Listening to the Bells: Learning to Read Poetry by Writing Poetry*. Portsmouth, NH: Boynton Cook, 1991.

Johnson, D. M. *Word Weaving: A Creative Approach to Teaching and Writing Poetry*. Urbana, IL: National Council of Teachers of English, 1990.

Karay, J. *Finger Fun-ics: A Collection of Finger Plays, Action Verses & Songs.* Bowling Green, KY: Kinder Kollege Press, 1995.

Lewis, R. *When Thought Is Young: Reflections on Teaching & the Poetry of the Child.* Minneapolis, MN: New River Press, 1992.

Lies, B.B. *The Poet's Pen: Writing Poetry with Middle and High School Students.* Englewood, CO: Teachers Ideas Press, 1993.

Mayfield, C. *Poetic License: In Poem and Song.* Beverly Hills, CA: Dove Books, 1996.

Moore, V. *The Pleasure of Poetry with and by Children: A Handbook.* Metuchen, NJ: Scarecrow Press, 1981.

Morice, D. *The Adventures of Dr. Alphabet: 104 Unusual Ways to Write Poetry in the Classroom & the Community.* New York: Teachers & Writers Collaborative, 1996.

Ottenstein, C. *The Poetry Fun Book.* Spring, TX: Counterpart Publishing, 1992.

Parsons, L. *Poetry, Themes & Activities: Exploring the Fun & Fantasy of Language.* Portsmouth, NH: Heinemann, 1992.

Potts, C. *Poetry Fun by the Ton with Jack Prelutsky.* Fort Atkinson, WI: Highsmith Press, 1995.

Rumi, J. *Feeling the Shoulder of the Lion: Poems & Teaching Stories from the Mathnaw.* Translated by C. Bark. Putney, VT: Threshold Books, 1991.

Sedgwick, F. *Read My Mind: Young Children, Poetry & Learning.* New York: Routledge, 1997.

Steinbergh, J. *Reading & Writing Poetry: A Guide for Teachers.* New York: Scholastic, 1992.

Tucker, S. *Animal Tails: Poetry & Art by Children.* Seattle: Whiteaker Press, 1997.

Williams, J. *Let Me Out!: Introducing Poetry to Elementary Students.* Pittsburgh, PA: Magnolia Press, 1994.

Wilson, L. *Write Me a Poem: Reading, Writing & Performing Poetry.* Portsmouth, NH: Heinemann, 1994.

Children

Adams, A. *A Pretzel of Peculiar Proportion*. New York: Shining Light Press, 1996.

Adedjouma, D., ed. *The Palm of My Heart: Poetry by African American Children*. New York: Lee & Low Books, 1996.

Agard, J., and G. Nichols, eds. *A Caribbean Dozen: Poems from Caribbean Poets*. Cambridge, MA: Candlewick Press, 1994.

Adoff, A. *My Black Me: A Beginning Book of Black Poetry*. New York: Puffin Books, 1995.

Angelou, M. *All God's Children Need Travel*. New York: Random House, 1997.

Arnold, H. *Of Ebony & Alabaster*. Akron, OH: Multicultural Publications, 1996.

Aylesworth, J. *Wake Up, Little Children: A Rise-&-Shine Rhyme*. New York: Simon & Schuster Children's Books, 1996.

Bagert, B. *Chicken Socks: And Other Contagious Poems*. Honesdale, PA: Boyds Mills Press, 1994.

Banta, M. H. *A Certain Voice: A Collection of Poems*. Enid, OK: Grasshopper Publishers, 1996.

Berger-Kiss, A. *Voices from the Earth/Voces de le Tierra: A Bilingual Anthology of Poetry*. Lake Oswego: Condor Books, 1996.

Berry, J. *Classic Poems to Read Aloud*. New York: Larousse Kingfisher Chambers, 1995.

Binch, C., illus. *Down by the River: Afro-Caribbean Rhymes, Games & Songs for Children*. New York: Scholastic, 1996.

Campion, C. *Latino Rainbow: Poems about Latino Americans*. Danbury, CT: Children's Press, 1994.

Chorao, K. *The Book of Giving: Poems of Thanks, Praise & Celebration*. New York: Dutton's Children's Books, 1995.

Cohen, J. W. *Grandmother's Happy Poems for Children*. Santa Fe: C.E. Winter Publishing, 1996.

Cowing, S., comp. *Fire in the Sea: An Anthology of Poetry & Art*. Honolulu, HI: University of Hawaii Press, 1996.

Duffy, C. A. *I Wouldn't Thank You for a Valentine: Poems for Young Feminists*. New York: Henry Holt, 1995.

Dyer, J. *Animal Crackers: A Delectable Collection of Pictures, Poems & Lullabies for the Very Young*. New York: Little, Brown & Co., 1996.

Grimes, N. *Danitra Brown Leaves Town*. New York: Lothrop, Lee & Shepard Books, 1997.

Hendricks, M. *Muslim Poems for Children*. Chicago: Kazi Publications, 1996.

Hill, S. *Poems Not to Be Missed*. Grawn, MI: Publishers Distribution Service, 1995.

Hoberman, M. A. *My Song Is Beautiful: Poems and Pictures in Many Voices*. New York: Little, Brown & Co., 1994.

Hopkins, L. B. *Blast Off! Poems about Space*. New York: HarperCollins, 1995.

Hurst, I. O. *My Kaleidoscope of Poetry & Stories*. Lebanon, OR: Gemstone Publishing, 1992.

Jaberski, S., selector. *Morning, Noon & Night: Poems to Fill Your Day*. Greenvale, NY: Mondo Publishers, 1996.

Kherdian, D. *Beat Voices: An Anthology of Beat Poetry*. New York: Henry Holt, 1995.

Lewis, J. P. *The Bookworm's Feast: A Potluck of Poems*. New York: Dial Books for Young Readers, 1996.

Livingston, M. C., selector. *Riddle-Me Rhymes*. Old Tappan, NJ: Simon & Schuster, 1994.

Macaulay, T. *Non-Violent Stories & Poems for Children*. Baltimore: Noble House, 1996.

Maldonado, J. M. *Esta Era una Vez: Once Upon a Time*. Grandview, MI: Jesus Maria Maldonado, 1994.

Martin, B., Jr. *Fire! Fire! Said Mrs. McGuire*. San Diego: Harcourt Brace, 1996.

Mathis, S. B. *Red Dog, Blue Fly: Football Poems*. New York: Puffin Books, 1995.

La Penta, M. *Music, Songs & Poems*. Edited by S. Evento. New York: Newbridge Communications, 1995.

Otten, C. *Months: A Book of Poems for Children*. New York: Lothrop, Lee & Shepard Books, 1997.

Rosen, M., comp. *A Spider Bought a Bicycle and Other Poems for Young Children*. New York: Larousse Kingfisher Chambers, 1995.

Rosenberg, L. *Earth-Shattering Poems*. New York: Henry Holt, 1995.

Sanders, A. M. *Alligators, Monsters & Cool School Poems*. Des Moines, IA: Leadership Publications, 1995.

Saxon, S. *Potpourri*. Leeds: Grady Sue Loftin Saxon, 1996.

Scott, C. *Riotous Rhymes for Children of All Ages*. Philadelphia: George T. Bissel Company, 1996.

Shannon, G. *Spring: A Haiku Story*. New York: Greenwillow, 1996.

Shaw, A. *Until I Saw the Sea: A Collection of Seashore Poems*. New York: Henry Holt, 1995.

Slier, D., ed. *Make a Joyful Sound: Poems for Children by African American Poets*. New York: Scholastic, 1996.

Springer, N. *Music of Their Hooves: Poems about Horses*. Honesdale, PA: Boyds Mills Press, 1994.

Walton, R. *What to Do When a Bug Climbs in Your Mouth and Other Poems to Drive You Buggy*. New York: Lothrop, Lee & Shepard Books, 1995.

Weisman, H. *What's Your Name? And Other Poems*. Carlisle, MA: Discovery Enterprises, 1995.

Windham, S., comp. *The Mermaid & Other Sea Poems*. New York: Scholastic, 1996.

Yolen, J. *Alphabestiary: Animal Poems from A to Z*. Honesdale, PA: Boyds Mills Press, 1995.

———. *How Beastly! A Menagerie of Nonsense Poems*. Honesdale, PA: Boyds Mills Press, 1994.

References

Calkins, L. *Living Between the Lines*. Portsmouth, NH: Heinemann, 1991.

Cecil, N. L. *For the Love of Language: Poetry for Every Learner*. Winnipeg, MB: Peguis Publishers, 1994.

Harste, J. C., V. A. Woodward, and C. L. Burke. *Language Stories and Literacy Lessons*. Portsmouth, NH: Heinemann, 1984.

King, M. L. "Language and learning for child watchers." In *Observing the Language Learner*, 19–38. Edited by A. Jagger and M. T. Smith-Burke. Newark, DE: International Reading Association, 1985.

Lytle, S. L., and M. Botel. *Frameworks for Literacy*. Portsmouth, NH: Heinemann, 1990.

Newman, J. M. "Insights from recent reading and writing research and their implications for developing whole language curriculum." In *Whole Language: Theory in Use*, 7–36. Edited by J. M. Newman. Portsmouth, NH: Heinemann, 1985.

Teale, W. "Language arts for the twenty-first century." In *Stories to Grow On*. Edited by J. Jensen. Portsmouth, NH: Heinemann, 1989.

Wells, G. *The Meaning Makers: Children Learning Language and Using Language to Learn*, 205–223. Portsmouth, NH: Heinemann, 1986.

——— ."Developing Literate Minds." Paper presented at the annual meeting of the American Educational Research Association, New Orleans, 1988.

Also from Nancy Lee Cecil
For the Love of Language: Poetry for Every Learner
Learning Magazine Teachers' Choice Award Winner

"…provides a year's worth of ideas…a valuable acquisition for any teacher of reading/writing at any grade level."
—*CM Magazine*

"I never felt I had a handle on teaching poetry. This book made a difference…It's good."
—*Consortium for Whole Brain Learning*

All children are natural poets—even those academically at-risk. In *For the Love of Language*, Nancy Lee Cecil shows how literacy scaffolds can release the poet within every child. *For the Love of Language*:

- introduces 61 literacy scaffolds for creating poems
- promotes reading, writing, listening, and speaking skills
- incorporates geography, social studies, and science, as well as language arts
- opens doors of expression that help children build self-esteem and confidence

Written primarily for children in grades 1–6, those who have had limited experiences with poetry, and those in the earliest stages of English-language acquisition, this book will inspire everyone to play with language.

176 pages
ISBN: 1-895411-87-4

ORDER FORM *Photocopy this form to order*

PLEASE SEND:

For the Love of Language

_____ copy/ies @ $17 each _____

Subtotal _____

Shipping and handling
$3 or 8%, whichever is greater _____

Subtotal _____

Canadian residents add 7% GST _____

TOTAL _____

❏ purchase order attached
❏ check enclosed
❏ please charge my ❏ VISA ❏ MasterCard

_____
card number   expiry date

_____
signature

DELIVER TO:

_____
name

_____
address

_____
city

_____
state/province   zip code/postal code

ORDER BY MAIL:
Peguis Publishers
100-318 McDermot Ave.
Winnipeg, Manitoba
Canada R3A 0A2
tel: 204-987-3500

CALL TOLL FREE:
1-800-667-9673

ORDER BY FAX:
1-204-947-0080

ORDER BY E-MAIL:
peguis@peguis.mb.ca

◢◢ **PEGUIS**